TH_ UNEXPECTED THINGS

Jane   29 June 2024

I pray you find a new level of intimacy with our Jesus here.

Luv

BY

CHANTAL RATCLIFFE

Chantal

xx

(Matt 6:33)

The Unexpected Things

Published by Chantal Ratcliffe

Cape Town, South Africa

armfulofscrolls@gmail.com

ISBN: 978-0-7961-4241-2
eISBN: 978-0-7961-4242-9

2 4 6 8 10 9 7 5 3 1

Scripture quotations are from the following translations: English Standard Version, marked ESV; Amplified Bible, marked AMP; New International Version, marked NIV; The Message, marked MSG and the New King James Version, marked NKJV. All emphasis within the scripture quotes are author's own.

Illustrations and Cover designed by Kayleigh Hunter
Layout by Boutique Books

Printed in Cape Town, South Africa.

ENDORSEMENTS

This book blessed my heart! Chantal is an anointed teacher who is able to explain complex truths in an easy-to-understand way. *The Unexpected Things* is beautifully written. Chantal's relatable storytelling, the truth of scripture and the power of her testimony will captivate you with its authenticity and vulnerability. The message of this book is deep, theologically rich and powerful. Its principles will strengthen your heart and inspire you towards incredible faith. I came away from this book deeply inspired and refreshed – and have no doubt that you will, too.

Roger Pearce, Regional Apostolic & Cluster Leader, Every Nation Southern Africa.

The Unexpected Things is theologically sound and draws principles from the Bible that are important for daily living. Chantal writes candidly about her life experiences and how God showed up amid very challenging circumstances. The book is true to its title. It ministers to a soul that has faced unexpected things in life. Reading this book is like going to therapy and then being challenged and encouraged by the Word of God. Jesus said: "In this world, you will have trouble. But take heart! I have overcome this world." This book captures the words of our Master so well and builds hope for a glorious future and a different perspective.

Simon Lerefolo, Senior Pastor, Every Nation Rosebank.

DEDICATION

This book is first and foremost dedicated to my Lord, whose faithfulness continues to leave me in utter awe. And then to my entire family: I love and treasure each one of you dearly.

A WORD OF THANKS

To my husband Stuart: You gave so generously and in so many ways to support this project! Thank you for the many pep talks along the way. You helped push me over the finish line! I couldn't have done this without you. I love you.

To my beautiful, blended family: Cayden, Tylan, Sarah, Matthew and Joshua. You add colour to my life and make it rich! Each one of you are a great source of joy and delight. I love you.

To Mom: Thank you for the copious loads of washing you did for us, so that I could finish this book. You are a pillar of support and I love you.

To Dad: Your prayers cover and carry this family! It's an unseen labour of love, but one that is seen in the fruit of our daily lives. I love you.

To my talented niece Kayleigh Hunter: Thank you for creating the beautiful cover and all the images. Your willingness to help with anything at any time is deeply appreciated. I love you.

To my mentors in Christ: You know who you are! I am so grateful for your continued input and encouragement. I continue to grow in Christ because of your leadership, friendship and love – thank you.

To my editor Katherine Graham: You were right! The process with you made the arrow sharper. Thank you.

CONTENTS

INTRODUCTION

Chapter 1:

THE UNEXPECTED THINGS

Benjamin Franklin famously said there are two certainties in this life – death and taxes. While I agree that death is indeed inevitable, in some countries (I write from my beloved South Africa), it appears to be quite possible to avoid paying a wide array of taxes altogether.

But let's not discuss politics! My purpose in raising this old adage is rather to add to it because I believe that there's one more thing we can count on as an absolute certainty in this life: we will all, most definitely, meet with the *unexpected things.*

You know the kind of events I'm talking about – those uninvited ones that suddenly appear and turn our world upside down, often bringing with them a pain so great it makes even our simplest of daily tasks seem difficult. These are the unexpected things you and I have the misfortune of facing in this life.

The unexpected things are unplanned. They are unwanted circumstances that creep up on us and disrupt our sense of stability. They are the kinds of events that catch us completely off guard and deal a hefty, debilitating blow.

Much like the one that upended my life in October 1997 when I discovered that my husband had a seven-year-old daughter with another woman. The discovery left me numb with shock as I tried to come to terms with what seemed like a cruel twist in a soap opera. Except this wasn't make-believe. This was really happening. And it was happening to *me.*

The day we'd stood at the altar and promised to love each other forever, my husband knew that he already had a child on the way with another woman. He'd kept his secret hidden from me from the beginning. What's worse is that his plan succeeded! For seven years he went on building a life and family with me as if absolutely nothing was amiss and for all those years he'd lived a double life, I was none the wiser.

Talk about the carpet being ripped out from under my feet! In truth, it felt more like the earth had just shifted in its axis as I tried to wrap my head around the extent of my husband's dishonesty and betrayal.

That was a long time ago, so long ago now that it seems to fit in another lifetime – someone else's life, really. And yet I remember sitting in my lounge in the early hours of the morning with tears streaming down my face as I prayed as if it were only yesterday.

I have personally experienced the unexpected things more times than I care to remember. And I am certain that if you and I could sit down to a cup of coffee together, you could tell me some stories of your own. Unexpected things happen and they happen to all of us.

The truth of it is that while the consequences of sin continue to abound in this fallen world, the unexpected things are here to stay and are as certain as death (Rom 1:28–32; 3:9–18). Yet unlike death, the unexpected can call on us more than once! There is no free pass on the unexpected things because we've had the misfortune of meeting it once before. In a way, the unexpected things can be much tougher for us than our eventual death because we must keep facing them, one devastating event after another, over and over again.

Because we don't anticipate meeting with the unexpected things in life, we're less likely to be prepared to meet them. Most people anticipate the event of their death and even go about preparing for it in a number of different ways. We set up life insurance policies, prepare a living will and make a number of other preparations for our loved ones for when we'll no longer be alive. Some of us even go to the extent of specifying what our memorial service will be like – what hymns will be sung and what flowers to decorate the church with. We have an entire industry organized around helping us with these preparations.

When it comes to our faith life, we also prepare spiritually for this eventuality. By receiving Jesus Christ as Lord and Saviour, we secure our eternity in His presence. Even as we walk out our daily relationship with Jesus, we are ensuring our continual readiness to meet with Him when we pass on from this natural world. The inevitability of our death is therefore always on our spiritual radar and quite central to the way we live out our faith in Christ.

We all *expect* at some point to meet with death. We rather hope that it comes much later in life and in a peaceful way, but nevertheless prepare for its inevitability. Not so when it comes to the unexpected things.

We tend to hope and pray that we will be one of the "lucky" or "blessed" ones who can somehow escape the unwelcome consequences of sin and the resulting trauma.

And yet we live in *this* world, a world that remains severely impacted by the Fall. Adam and Eve's decision to disobey God ushered into His creation death, something it had never known before (Gen 3). Plunging both humanity and creation into devastating consequences (Rom 8:19–23; John 17:15–16; 1 John 2:16). Consequences that are only increasing and intensifying as corrupted humanity continues to sin[1]. These effects are easily seen in the world today (Rom 1:28–32; 3:10–18; Gal 5:19–21; Jas 1:15).

Our reluctance to accept the inevitability of the unexpected things means that we also don't really think about preparing spiritually for them. We don't prepare our faith to meet the unexpected things because we don't expect them to happen to us. Oh, we know that they happen. We even admit that they are currently happening to others. But we don't expect that they will happen to *us*. (This cognitive bias is well recognised and is known by psychologists as the optimism bias.)

The result of this unpreparedness means that as believers, our faith tends to get derailed when disaster strikes. The unexpected things don't just affect our natural lives, they can also upend our spiritual lives. To demonstrate this, we need only look as far as the shores of shipwrecked faith, those whose faith has run aground by the unexpected things. Perhaps you know of someone like this. Perhaps that someone is you?

We face some of our greatest personal faith challenges when meeting with an unanticipated crisis. These events test our faith like nothing else will and can strand us for years in a place of confusion and doubt.

The unexpected things ask some very big questions of our faith and test our belief and trust in a loving and faithful God. And whenever our faith finds itself in a perplexing place where it has more questions than it knows what to do with, never mind attempting to find answers, it is completely immobilised.

As a result, our faith is never more vulnerable and our destiny never more at risk than when the unexpected things strike. These trying circumstances place a huge demand on our faith at a time when we least expect it.

The force of the unexpected is its element of surprise. And it is not the good kind of surprise: a surprise party, a gift with your name on it or fortuitously winning a prize. Rather, it is that thunderbolt kind of surprise. The take-ten-years-off-our-life kind of surprise! Its impact forces us to travel into the territory of the unfamiliar and unknown. Here our faith must try to navigate an unpredictable environment left in the wake of devastation.

This is already a lot for our faith to be dealing with, but it is not the full extent of it. During a crisis, we are often called upon to make important choices, even life-altering ones. All these decisions will ultimately impact our life and destiny in Christ. And we must do this under the immense strain of raw emotional pain. This is a tall order for our faith. Just think back to the last time you faced the unexpected things and remember how it felt to get your head around your new reality, never mind plot an immediate course through it!

But there is still more. Nothing plays more into the hands of the enemy to shake our trust in God than the unexpected things. These traumatic events quickly expose our vulnerabilities, presenting the devil with the kinds of opportunity he has been waiting for (Matt 4:2–4).

Yes, the unexpected things happen to us all and can take the wind right out of our faith sails. In these moments, many of us are sorely tempted to become disillusioned with both God and His promises. And far too often this leads us to suspend, if not abandon, our ongoing intimacy with Him. Haven't we all experienced disillusioned faith to some degree? I certainly have.

The unexpected things are confusing and disorientating. When we meet them unprepared, our faith cannot remain steadfast, make critical decisions, deal with the devil and hold fast to God.

Let's return to the idea of the inevitability of death. Consider for a moment that unlike death, there is no industry organised around helping us prepare for the certainty of the unexpected things. What we do have is a robust industry built around helping us pick up all the devastating pieces *after* a disaster has smashed through our lives. Take, for example, the services of the mental health industry and its vast array of medicine and therapy designed to keep us from spiralling into the abyss of despair. Our churches also provide wonderful counselling programmes that offer support for those who are dealing with crises.

Don't get me wrong – mental healthcare and counselling are important and a gift to all of us who need them. But it does leave me wondering if we might be dealing with the inevitability of unexpected things with a bit of a lopsided approach.

Given the enormous potential for our faith to run aground in times of crisis, shouldn't we be looking at ways to prepare ourselves as best we can to meet them? Surely this would be a better strategy than to merely hope that we don't ever meet with the unexpected things, only then to be shattered when we eventually do?

Put differently, if we don't prepare our faith for the unexpected things, we're settling for a perpetual cycle of spiritual upheaval every time we do meet with one. Choosing to expose our faith to vulnerability is far worse than diligently preparing it in anticipation of times of crisis (Prov: 22:3).

Unprepared, we tend to feel defenceless in the face of the difficult circumstances that confront us when the unexpected happens in our lives. But it doesn't have to be this way.

Our victory is not found in the absence of adversity. Life will change and does change all the time. No matter who you are, what title you hold, what you do to earn a living or where you are in your spiritual walk with God – unexpected things happen. If we are to thwart the enemy's schemes against our faith and destiny in times of crisis, we need to tip the scales in favour of preparedness.

We can plan for the unplanned. It seems an anomaly, I know, but God wants us to prepare for these eventualities by equipping ourselves with the tools our faith needs, so that we can not only meet them, but prevail against them (Eph 6:10–19). This is the victory we have access to through our Lord and Saviour, Jesus Christ!

In this book, I explore some of the ways we can do just that: prepare our faith to meet the unexpected things. Together we will consider the inevitability of the unexpected things in our lives, as well as our common responses to them. A great deal can be learned from our responses when we juxtapose them with godly men and women.

In the Scriptures, we will find some sturdy handles for our faith to hold fast to during turbulent times. These will support us as we journey through the many unknowns that are synonymous with the unexpected things. Just knowing that our faith has a handle it can rely on for support during these trials brings a measure of comfort to our hearts. But these handles give us so much more than confidence. They help us remain spiritually steadfast at a time when everything threatens to give way.

It is my hope that as we explore this topic together, you will come to recognise the inevitability of the unexpected things and start working to prepare your faith for them. I pray that you will be better equipped to navigate your way through these hard seasons in life without your faith being shipwrecked, without letting go of God's hand or losing communion with His Spirit. The Bible shows us the way to move through our confusing and disorientating times. But before we move on to look at these things, I want to take a moment to encourage you.

You might be experiencing a painful crisis right now. You may already feel disillusioned with God and His promises and be on the verge of giving up. Perhaps at the nudge of the Holy Spirit or the recommendation of a loved one, you opened this book as your last hope – your final attempt to find God's kindness amid your present difficulties.

Wherever you may be, I want to urge you not to let go of your Heavenly Father's hand. Jesus loves you! He has promised to never leave you (Heb: 13:5). I know that what you are going through is painful and confusing. I know that you have more questions for God than answers. I, too, have been in these depths of confusion and distress – more than once, in fact.

But I have specifically prayed for you. I truly believe that as you read this book, you will again discover that the hand you want to let go of right now is a loving, kind one and the right one to grab hold of. God is the only One that can bring you through this awful place and into the victory He has secured for you through His Son, Jesus.

So, please don't let go. Don't give up on Him just yet. Keep turning these pages and let's trust God together that nestled somewhere in the midst of them is the very help and encouragement you need right now.

Chapter 2:

THE BIGGER PICTURE

When It Doesn't Make Any Sense

I had no idea my first husband was living a dual life. I didn't expect my entire marriage to be built on such a hideous lie, nor for my two sons to be born into such a shambles. So, what do we do when life doesn't go according to plan? And more importantly, how do we frame these crises in the context of our relationship with a loving God?

I have discovered when it comes to understanding our situation from a faith perspective, particularly with circumstances that don't make sense, it's often due to a barrier, much like the one I encountered on a trip to South Korea many years ago.

In South Korea, I encountered something I'd never experienced before. When I travel, I thoroughly enjoy engaging and connecting with locals; it's a wonderful way to get to know and experience a new culture. I had a similar expectation, albeit uninformed, for my visit to South Korea. However, it soon became apparent that most of the locals didn't speak a word of English and even when I did find someone who could, I wasn't able to get much further than, "How are you?"

The language barrier made finding my way around Seoul daunting. I couldn't ask anyone for directions – but this did not stop me from trying! Refusing to be put off by people shaking their heads at me, I persisted in asking one South Korean after another if they spoke English. Surely there was one?

Apart from the disappointment of not being able to talk to anyone, I was severely limited in the extent to which I could be adventurous and discover new things. Finding the right buses to take, for example, was simply impossible. All the signage was in Korean, with absolutely no English to be found anywhere. I was terrified I would end up on the wrong bus. With no way to communicate, how would I ever find my way back?

Similarly, our God-given destiny in Christ, is uncovered in an environment that is completely different to the one we live in. Ours is a natural, worldly environment and His a spiritual, heavenly one. To borrow an analogy from my South Korean experience, you and I speak fluent "natural" and when we seek to understand the ways of God with our lives, particularly when our circumstances don't make any sense, our fluent "natural" immediately meets a barrier that we have to overcome.

The Bigger Picture

The first thing we need to understand is that there is a much bigger picture for our lives than the one we have sight of. This bigger picture is the substance of God's sovereignty. This means that He alone holds the blueprint for your life and has designed your days according to the counsel of His will (Eph 1:11).

His plans for us unfold according to this design and on a much larger scale, the greater part of which for us remains unseen. Because of this, when it comes to reconciling our situations with our faith, you and I need help.

I'm shortsighted and I can't see very far: everything in the distance is blurred and out of focus. My eyes need help to bring what is in the distance – what my natural vision can see – into clear focus and so I wear prescription glasses.

Without my glasses, I can get by (at a push), but I simply cannot see things clearly or in any detail. Similarly, when it comes to looking at our life through God's eyes (our eyes of faith), we too need a visual aid. We need a lens to keep the bigger picture in view. We find it in Isaiah 55:8–9 (ESV):

> For my thoughts are not your thoughts, neither are your ways my ways, declares the Lord. For as the heavens are higher than the earth, so are my ways higher than your ways and my thoughts than your thoughts.

Here in Isaiah 55, God is revealing His heart for humanity and reminding His people of His universal mission to bring the whole world to salvation[2]. In this regard, He wants them to see that His plans and thoughts for humanity are far greater than their narrow vision. This principle has a much broader application when we juxtapose God's vastness against our human limitations.

Simply put, God's ways are higher than ours. Although we acknowledge this truth, we often fail to *apply* it when we try to interpret what He's doing in our lives. There is a big difference between discovered truth (what we know) and applied truth (what we practise). This same difference is often what determines our spiritual success or failure.

When we fail to apply the principle of Isaiah 58:8 to our circumstances, we experience our journey in Christ much the same way I experience my surroundings when I don't wear my glasses – we might get by, but we certainly won't see things clearly. And when we don't see properly, we're unable to accurately interpret our circumstances within the bigger picture of God's purposes.

Framing our lives from God's perspective is very important because He alone knows the course He has set for each of us and is always moving us towards this end. As we follow Christ, we might be planning our way through this world, but He is the One ultimately *directing* our steps according to His blueprint (Prov 16:9). This is the principle of the bigger picture that governs the life of a believer.

I recently returned from a trip to Singapore with my husband. We visited Sentosa Island where we went riding on the Luge. First, we had to take a fairly lengthy ski lift up to the starting point which was at the top of a steep slope. From there, we raced down various tracks on sleds with wheels. It was terrific fun! Our tickets allowed us multiple rides, so we had to take the ski lift up the slope over and over again. It was the only way to get to the start to experience the thrill of the ride.

The truth of this verse is a bit like that ski lift. We need to let it take us up to the starting point or, in this case, the correct viewpoint, when trying to interpret how our messy lives relate to His sovereign plan.

The more time we spend gazing through this lens and applying the principle of this verse to our lives, the more accustomed we become to the many shades of its truth.

The Seen and The Unseen

> "... we do not look at the things which are seen, but at the things which are not seen. For the things which are seen are temporary, but the things which are not seen are eternal" (2 Cor 4:18 NKJV).

Life has trained us exclusively for our earthly environment. We are accustomed to this seen world. (Remember the earlier example of trying to talk to someone in a language they don't understand?) As a result, we tend to ignore the spiritual realm. Our life plans are made for this world, a world the Bible clearly tells us is temporary.

We put enormous effort into our lives here. We get a decent education, so that we can become employable in order to secure a good job. We plan to earn a steady income, so that we can provide for those we love. We know that our decisions are important, so we try to make good ones to prepare ourselves for the very best. We plan and plan and plan and exert a tremendous amount of energy towards achieving these goals.

We plan for tangible results and in all this planning, we plan for good. We plan according to our expectation for good things to happen; we don't plan for the bad. Yet as we well know, bad things happen to all of us. This is how we move through life: planning in this seen world. Our plans make sense to us because we think we know what the ultimate destination is.

By contrast, God has a spiritual plan for our lives, one we can't see. While this plan does include a period of life on earth, it continues way beyond that into eternity, reducing our life here to a mere fragment at best. His multidimensional plan unfolds in the spiritual, unseen world. In that eternal context, His plans make absolute sense because He knows what the end goal is.

Here lies the chasm between the two sets of plans. The seen and known versus the unseen and unknown. Both are real. Both are important. So how do we reconcile the two? What can lift our understanding beyond our natural tendency to focus on what is seen, tangible and known?

To do this, we will need the help of a different filter.

Join The Dots

Do you remember those join-the-dot activity sheets we did as kids? You were given a page filled with lots of numbered dots and your task was to join them in numerical order with a pencil. You would methodically connect the dots, searching the page for the next sequential number. Eventually, having joined the dots from beginning to end, you would discover the picture it revealed.

I remember loving doing these exercises because beyond the seemingly random mass of dots, there was a very specific picture and each join-the-dot activity revealed a different one. Sometimes it was a flower, an animal or a train. Each join-the-dot page took my imagination on a journey of discovery. What picture was buried beneath the chaotic spray of dots?

I remember how my sons when they were young also enjoyed doing these activities. No sooner had they started connecting the dots than they would launch into a guessing game of what the uncovered picture would be. Each of them would shout out the names of various things they thought it might be. They couldn't stop until their curiosity had been satisfied.

It may have been a long time since you did a join-the-dot activity sheet or watched a child do one. Usually once it was done, we would colour it in, write our names on it and then… ta-da! The big moment would arrive when we proudly presented it to our parents to stick up on the fridge. Grinning from ear to ear, we would bask in their praises of how beautiful our picture was, even when the rhino was missing both its horn and eye because we skipped over numbers 20 to 25!

If you are in anyway connected to a young child, you will know that parents have a place in their home displaying these "works of art". It is usually a fridge door or what used to look like a fridge door, but is now a collage of drawings with bits protruding over the edges. And yes, most of them are either unidentifiable or missing key parts!

That wasn't important to us as children. What mattered is that our parents celebrated our childish achievements. Whether we completed the picture or not, our effort went up on the fridge and was cherished as a masterpiece and it felt so good, remember?

This simple childhood activity gives us a useful tool in bridging the chasm between the seen and the unseen. It's also handy when it comes to applying the truth of Isaiah 55:8–9 to the things that just don't make sense to us.

Imagine that the bigger picture of God's blueprint for your life looked similar to an epic join-the-dots activity. There is a dot that marks both the beginning and the end of your journey and beneath the myriad dots lies a very detailed picture waiting to be revealed for all eternity.

It's your personal page of destiny in Christ and nobody else but you can uncover the picture it holds. Your dots have been designed in divine sequence and your assignment is to connect them in the right order, so that you can uncover the eternal picture – without any pieces missing.

Using this simple illustration reveals some important spiritual truths. When we grab hold of these insights and really make them ours, our faith will become more adept at correctly framing our unplanned and seemingly nonsensical circumstances within the bigger picture of God's eternal purposes.

Chapter 3:

MY OWN DOT JOURNEY

Considering life as an epic join-the-dots activity quickly triggers our interest and brings our own journey to the fore. And if your imagination is at all like mine, your mind has already grabbed hold of the image of a page filled with dots and you are itching to connect them to see what picture it will uncover!

But first, we must pause to consider something important when it comes to how we draw the connecting lines. As children, we simply had to pick up a pencil and work methodically through the chain of numbers, but as Christ followers walking out our lives, it's a lot more complex.

Now our daily life is the pencil with which we draw the connecting lines. Our choices determine the dot sequence. And the stakes are much higher. Your personal page of destiny holds a picture that only your life can uncover and its completion carries the weight of eternity.

This is a sobering thought and rightfully so, for the spiritual implications are significant. You see, when we were children, it didn't matter if we skipped over dots or connected them in the wrong order. But in this instance, with eternity in full view, it does matter. And it matters a great deal.

Just as every numbered dot on a join-the-dots activity has value in its eventual completion, so each dot in our lives contributes to the ultimate, eternal whole of it. Every dot of our life story holds spiritual significance and consequences, both here and in eternity. Therefore, a lot depends on the way we live our lives on earth.

Simply put, a life lived is a picture drawn. There are no do-overs. There is no going back after death to erase and redraw some of our connecting lines or make any last-minute changes to our picture. Hence the exhortation in scripture to "walk circumspectly, not as fools but as wise, redeeming the time, because the days are evil" (Eph 5:15–16 NKJV).

We are exhorted to embrace the kind of wisdom that recognises the significance of every dot in our lives. For when we reach the final dot and go to be with the Lord, our lifetime will most certainly uncover a picture – whether the rhino is sporting its horn or not.

Mercifully, a life in progress is a drawing still in progress. There is still time for us to examine how we are living before God on earth and reset our lives if necessary. Now is the time to consider the importance of our daily life with regard to the bigger picture and make any required adjustments. Today, we must determine to let God work freely in and through our lives as we sketch out our eternal, one-of-a-kind picture for His glory.

To live a life that will bring glory to God is not something we can do by ourselves. Unlike our childhood activity sheets, we can't see the numbers on all our dots. Imagine I put a join-the-dots activity before you without any numbers on the dots – how on earth would you know which dot connects with which? None of us would even attempt such a task because we know we need the sequence to solve the puzzle.

When it comes to our personal dot journey, only God knows the divine order of our dots. Only His Spirit can help us connect our dots in the right sequence. Only He knows the what, where, why, who and how of our God-breathed destiny.

Continually before us is that ever-present barrier separating our seen world from His unseen realm. In the vast difference between them lie the infinite unknowns we must constantly grapple with in this life. Do I go left or right here? Should I do this or that? And so it goes on.

When everything is going well and we have relative calm in our lives, we at least have the luxury of not needing to find immediate answers for our unknowns. But when it comes to the unexpected things, this is simply not the case.

A crisis doesn't give us the opportunity to figure everything out. In this place, time is of the essence and the chasm between the visible and invisible looms larger than ever before.

Suddenly, the unknowns become significantly scarier. Crushed with the weight of our crisis, we must now make important decisions. A direction must be chosen. A line must be drawn to connect the dots. And it's often here that we find ourselves at a total loss as to what to do next.

A million thoughts ran through my mind that night, all those years ago, as I sat processing my first husband's devastating betrayal. I was already dealing with the difficult reality of being married to an alcoholic who was in total denial of his addiction and its resulting consequences to me and our two small boys.

I was barely keeping my prayerful head above these stormy waters and now, on top of all of this, was the discovery that he had another child with another woman. And this child was as old as our marriage was! It was too much.

As devastated as I was, I also felt compassion for this seven-year-old girl and grieved by the injustice of keeping her away from her father and family as if *she* was the mistake. I grieved that this precious little girl had become the victim, something to hide, because of the actions of her parents. I grieved because so many had not been given the opportunity to celebrate her arrival, as it deserved to be celebrated. I wept for all her losses and I remember a fierce desire to set things right for her – as far as I was able to.

My thoughts then turned to my sons and my heart broke into a million shattered pieces. They were still so young, one a toddler and the other barely five years old. This news would impact their lives significantly, even though they wouldn't be able to understand it fully. How would I go about sharing the news with them. What would I say and how should I say it? What if the mother of this child (who was a complete stranger to me) was lying and this little girl was not really my husband's daughter after all?

What do I do for my sons now and how do I do it the right way, with their best interests at heart? How do I protect them from harm through all of this?

I sat there, alone with Jesus, in the early hours of the morning, my mind racing with these questions. And I wept. I wept for my husband's daughter. I wept for my sons. And I wept for all the brokenness that was spilling into our lives.

My thoughts turned from one direction to another, as I sought His comfort and counsel. I wept for the great devastation this sin had caused and the harsh consequences it brought as I prayed for wisdom as to what to do next.

Surprisingly enough, I wasn't angry. Anger didn't feature anywhere in my heart that night. Instead, there was a deep sense of grief and pain in my soul. I was sure that if I could take my heart out to look at it, it would lay bruised and bleeding in the palm of my hand.

But I didn't have time to wait for that pain to subside, so that I could start living again. I had to make decisions. I was in pain, but I had to function and I had to function well because I had two small children relying on me.

I was acutely aware that the decisions I had to make would not only impact my life, but the many lives (and generations) associated with this regrettable situation. I somehow knew that the line I chose to draw here would connect us all in a dot sequence that would impact my marriage, my sons, this little girl, her mother, our parents and the broader families. And I felt the immense weight of this responsibility before God. What would bring Him glory through this brokenness?

After sitting for many hours in this posture of prayer, I finally asked the Lord to show me how He wanted me to respond in this situation. I became fully aware that my reactions were just as important as my actions before Him and I wanted to react according to His Spirit, not my flesh. He alone knew how to move all those involved in this situation with the least amount of hurt and I wanted His solution for each of us.

I didn't get much sleep that night and what's worse is that the next day, I had to move through the motions of daily life as if the last 12 hours had never happened for the sake of my sons. This continued for weeks afterwards.

I still had to get up and go to work every morning and I still had to parent my children. I couldn't simply resign from these daily activities and take time out to process everything. Life didn't stop when this crisis hit my life, even if it felt to me as if it should have. Life goes on and I had to keep getting up every morning and keep functioning as usual, even though on the inside I was devastated.

Have you ever seen someone crush an empty can in one hand? The weeks that followed the revelation of my husband's infidelity felt a lot like that for me – as if the hand of my crushing circumstances were squeezing the very life out of me.

The unexpected things have the power to crumple our lives like that can. Under the force of our crushing circumstances, the structure we normally rely on threatens to give way. And for some of us, it does just that – caves in.

Our spiritual lives also feel the crushing grip of this hand. Even our routine practices of Bible reading, prayer and worship feel clumsy and laboured or worse – stop altogether. The framework of our normal spiritual practice seems to want to give way under the extreme pressure we find ourselves in.

Yet this framework is desperately needed in these times. We can't afford to have it cave in, for it is the critical infrastructure which our faith needs to function. We walk by faith and so we desperately need our faith to remain strong and intact under the weight of what we're facing (2 Cor 5:7).

If this critical infrastructure caves in, we won't be able to respond by the Spirit in the unexpected places. This is crucially important – to walk as He leads, not by the flesh. For our responses in these hard places have manifold consequences, both eternally and for the generations to come.

Navigating those ensuing weeks was like a terrifying experience I had as a teenager driving home one night. I hadn't had my driver's licence for long and had gone out to meet with some friends. Hours later, we left to go home and discovered that a dense fog had settled on us. I couldn't see more than a few metres ahead of me. It was eerie.

I was anxious because after eventually finding my car in the parking lot, I had to attempt to drive home on my own. With a dose of youthful courage, I set off driving at a snail's pace in the general direction of home, roughly an 18km trip. It was a terrifying experience. I couldn't see where I was going.

I inched my way through this thick fog. Other cars only became visible when they were literally on top of me. My lights weren't much help either and seemed to do nothing more than prove just how little of my surroundings I could actually see.

I kept hoping that I would eventually break through the fog into a clearing – a gap of some sort – so that I could try to spot a familiar landmark. At least then I could get my bearings, which would have bolstered my confidence that I was heading in the right direction. But with every kilometre I managed to drive, the fog remained just as dense and scary. I never did come into any sort of clearing.

The drive home that night was long and scary. And when I did finally pull into my driveway, I couldn't even see the gate through the fog. I had to get out the car to feel around for the gate and open it, before driving the car safely in.

The fact that it was so late at night and that I was alone heightened my sense of terror. Back then, we didn't have the modern convenience of cell phones and finding a telephone booth given the circumstances wasn't an option. I couldn't simply call my father to come out and help me. No, this journey I had to do alone – in the thickest of fogs - like the journey through the weeks following my husband's betrayal.

Thankfully, I've only experienced fog like that once in my driving life. I can't, however, say the same for my faith life. In the unexpected places, my faith has often found itself engulfed in a thick haze of confusion and finding my way through it has been equally unsettling.

Navigating through the unexpected feels a lot like that experience I had as a teenager. We find ourselves engulfed in a thick fog of unwanted circumstances. Many unknowns surround us. We can scarcely see a way forward and our crushing circumstances serve as a continual reminder of just how powerless we are.

On top of that, in the midst of this confusion, our faith must work. Not only must our faith maintain the routine of spiritual practices, but here in the thickest of fogs, our spiritual senses must be alert, so that we can follow the leading of the Holy Spirit and connect the right dots together.

Choosing to respond by the Spirit in a crisis seems an insurmountable faith challenge. It is indeed difficult; the crisis places will test the quality and depth of our spiritual infrastructure like nothing else will. That's why we must prepare our faith ahead of time.

Let's now look at some ways we can strengthen this critical infrastructure, so that when we do meet the unexpected things, our indispensable faith doesn't cave in under pressure.

SECTION 1:
HANDLE OF PARTNERSHIP

"Since this is the kind of life we have chosen, the life of the Spirit, let us make sure that we do not just hold it as an idea in our heads or a sentiment in our hearts, but work out its implications in every detail of our lives."
(Gal 5:25 MSG)

God did not abandon us to navigate the fog of our crises alone. He sent us the help we need – a partner. And this is no ordinary partner, but rather the third co-equal of the Triune Godhead, the precious Holy Spirit – in other words, God Himself. This means that when we meet the fog of the unexpected things, we have God Himself as our resident partner to help guide us through it. This is good news!

A handle has many uses. It's something we can hold onto for support and it is also something we use to open a door with. A handle offers us both *support* and *access*. When it comes to navigating our way through the unexpected things, these two elements are indispensable to our faith. The first handle we will look at, what I call the Handle of Partnership, equips our faith with both of them.

When we meet crushing circumstances, we need support. If our faith has nothing against which it can bolster itself, it might collapse. We don't want that. We want our faith to remain steadfast when we meet the inevitability of the unexpected things. We want to be counted among the overcomers – those who go on to overcome through these hardships, not among those who have succumbed to the force of them (Rev 21:7).

Support for our faith through these difficulties is essential, but of equal importance is access. When we find ourselves engulfed in a thick fog, we desperately need to find a way forward. Our arm of faith must be able to reach beyond the barriers of our natural understanding and access the mind of God to uncover the path He has laid out for us. Without being able to find this critical information, we're left sorting through all our unknowns by ourselves, which is about as much help to us as my lights were that night when I drove home alone through the dense fog. Fortunately for me, I knew the way home, but when we face crises, it's a very different story. Thankfully, God doesn't leave us to depend on ourselves alone: He sent us a partner.

The partnership of the Holy Spirit is the ultimate game changer in our lives. Jesus experienced this personally. He knew the great significance and value of this partnership. It was the Spirit who empowered him throughout His earthly ministry and we see the evidence of this divine partnership in every facet of His ministry: in every miracle Jesus performed, in His death on the cross, His resurrection from the dead and His ascension into heaven.

So yes, Jesus by His own experience knew that partnership with the Holy Spirit was essential in our lives, which is why He was most eager to send Him to us (John 16:7). The Lord knew that without this critical partnership, we wouldn't be appropriately equipped to do what He has called us to do (Luke 24:49).

By sending us the Holy Spirit, the Lord set us up in the greatest partnership we could ever experience here on earth. And by it, He successfully gave us full access to the power of God at all times (John 16:13–15). This is very good news for those of us who are in Christ, for there is no other way to access the power of God – only by His Spirit. Think about that for a moment: you are filled with the Spirit of God and through Him you have full access to the power of the Triune Godhead. Wow! Talk about the ultimate game changer when it comes to connecting all our dots.

Our partner is the very Spirit of Jesus Christ and longs to guides us (Phil 1:19; John 16:13). He is the Spirit of wisdom who reveals the things of God to us and the only one on earth that can make known the things God has prepared for us (Eph 1:17; 1 Cor 2: 12). He "searches everything, even the depths of God" and knows the very "thoughts of God" concerning our life (1 Cor 2:10-11 ESV). He holds all this valuable information and what's more, He's eager to disclose it all to us (1 Cor 2:9–12). He is a willing and fully invested partner, just the kind we need when our lives meet the unexpected. Let's face it, could we find any better than God Himself as our partner when the fog settles down over our lives and we need to see what lies beyond? I don't think so.

The Holy Spirit is the greatest partner we could ever have. He is the very power of God in our lives. What's more, He does all the heavy lifting. He carries the lion's share of our partnership endeavours. When it comes to navigating our way through the fog, His help is indispensable. The Spirit can always see what we can't. The fog of our confusing circumstances doesn't limit His vision, even when it limits ours. He knows which dot you are at right now and He longs to lead you onto the next one.

Sadly, there is often a big disconnect between this truth and the lived experiences of many Christ followers. For many of us, this valuable partnership lies mostly dormant in our daily lives. That's not to say we have never experienced His partnership. We couldn't have received Jesus Christ as Lord and Saviour without His help (John 16:7–11). Yet, for the most part, we visit this partnership more than we actively stay in it. We visit for different reasons and for varying lengths of time, depending on what our need is. This was not what the Lord intended our interaction with His Spirit to be (Gal 5:25). He was not sent as the spare wheel in our lives, someone we turn to only when what we've been relying on gives in. He was sent as the engine, the One who continually powers our daily lives.

The first disciples understood this truth on the day of Pentecost. The power of God, revealed by His indwelling Spirit, completely transformed their lives and ministries, the results of which we see in the New Testament. For the early church, active partnership with the Spirit was normal Christian life. It wasn't something extraordinary that only the spiritually mature knew; it was everyday Christianity. These disciples knew that placing their trust in Christ meant placing their life at risk. Every day was a matter of life or death, so there was no way they could attempt to follow Jesus without depending entirely upon the Holy Spirit. It was partnership with the Spirit that led the disciples to smuggle Saul out of Damascus and later prevented some from preaching the gospel in Asia (Acts 9:25; 16:6). And there are umpteen similar examples recorded in Acts.

This call to receive and be continually filled with the Holy Spirit, to lean entirely upon Him, is a central theme found throughout the New Testament (Acts 8:17; 19:2; Rom 8:14; Eph 5:18; Gal 5:25; 6:8). It was consistently taught by the early church leaders. Not only were they faithful in living it as an example to all, they also took great care to document its importance, thereby safeguarding this truth for all believers.

We have been given a tremendous gift in the partnership of His Spirit. To walk in the Spirit and be led by the Spirit implies a dynamic partnership. It requires active participation. We can't prepare our faith to meet with the unexpected things without maintaining a vibrant partnership with the Holy Spirit. In a crisis, there is simply no way to respond by the Spirit unless we are well practised in what it means to work with Him.

Therefore, the first step in planning for the unplanned is to become *active* partners.

It requires a decision to move away from inaction, to no longer be satisfied with just occasionally visiting this partnership. It requires an intentionality to pursue close and intimate daily fellowship with Him. Our opening scripture from The Message captures the essence of this partnership so well. To be led by the Spirit is something much more than "an idea in our heads or a sentiment in our hearts". Rather, it's the substance of a vibrant union that permeates "every detail of our lives" (Gal 5:25). Selah.

He already knows what picture your life is going to uncover, He knows what lies behind all those unconnected dots and He is poised to partner with you. He will lead you from one dot to the next, at the right time and in the right order. He will lead you through the fog of the unknowns in life and the devastation of the unexpected. But this invitation to team with Him necessitates a very specific response from you – your cooperation.

Chapter 4:

THE CALL TO COOPERATION

"... a king... sent his servants to call those who were invited..."

(Matt 22:2–3 ESV)

The word "cooperation" is defined by the Oxford dictionary as "the process of working together to the same end"[3]. The notion of working together towards the same end implies active and continual partnership. Our response to the invitation to team up with the Spirit requires a steady posture of working together with Him toward His end. That end includes our God-given destiny in Christ, the final picture uncovered by our join-the-dots drawing. Our individual pictures all interconnect in the grand design of His Kingdom – your life is a critical piece that must be fitted into His overall divine puzzle.

Cooperation with God is the very essence of our salvation. Cooperation in partnership with Him is a theme expressed throughout the Scriptures. Men and women were called, at different times and for different reasons, to cooperate with God to achieve His divine purposes.

In partnership together, the Triune Godhead (Father, Son and Spirit) created the heavens and the earth (Gen 1:1; John 1:1). In partnership, God governed the garden with the first human beings – Adam and Eve, but this partnership was broken with the Fall and man literally fell out of cooperation with God. What a disastrous dot connection that was! If you needed any further convincing about the interconnectedness of our dot journeys, then look no further: Adam and Eve drew a connecting line that is still impacting the whole of humanity today.

God's subsequent redemptive plan for His fallen creation unfolds against this narrative of two-way partnership. Abraham, Moses, Mary and countless others received this invitation to cooperate with Him towards His redemptive end. It's a theme that starts off small and keeps developing as we move on through the Scriptures. God uses the cooperation of one man – Abraham – as the means to secure an entire nation, Israel, who can work together with Him.

It was a shadow of what was to come through Christ. What began with one man – Jesus of Nazareth, working in full cooperation with God's Spirit to accomplish His purposes, is now the means to God's end of securing a church who will cooperate with His eternal purposes. And today, as believers, it remains our mission to keep adding to this expanding company as we stay in cooperation with Him to "go and make disciples of all nations" (Matt 28:19). Great power for kingdom advancement is released through the cooperation of a single person: so much so that it remains the enemy's number one strategy to severe your cooperation with God.

By receiving Jesus Christ as Lord and Saviour, we come into partnership with God for His divine purposes. We have all received the call to cooperation with His Spirit and this call requires action. If we remain passive, there can be no working together. We are called into a partnership that requires us to be fully present ("follow Me" (Matt 16:24)), and fully engaged ("go" and "do" (Matt 28:19; Jas 1:22)) with His kingdom purposes in mind. This gives us a good picture of what working together with God looks like.

The great value in the help of the Holy Spirit is only unlocked through our ongoing cooperation with Him. Re-read that sentence because it is important. Many of us don't know the great benefit of the Spirit's help because we are sleeping partners. If we are to experience His tremendous value in our daily lives, we must wake up and start the work of cooperating with Him. It's no fun playing tennis with someone if the ball never comes back to you – in fact, it defeats the whole objective. When it comes to cooperation with the Spirit, how many "unreturned balls" are lying on our side of the court? If we are to realise the full benefit of our partner, we must be reliable and keep returning His balls. The work of joining all our dots in the right sequence depends on it.

Most of us sincerely desire to cooperate with the Holy Spirit, but we nevertheless find it challenging to work together with Him. We relate to God both corporately as the Body of Christ and individually. Our personal walk with the Holy Spirit is unique and dynamic because each of us are created differently. Consequently, our personal partnership with the Spirit presents different challenges to each of us.

It's useful to consider some important characteristics of cooperation. When we can identify what might be hindering our effective teamwork with God's Spirit, we are better equipped to make the necessary adjustments. In this way, the true work of familiarising our arm of faith with our heavenly partner can begin.

1. COOPERATION IS MORE THAN RELATIONSHIP

"Do you not know that in a race all the runners run (their very best to win), but only one receives the prize? Run (your race) in such a way that you may seize the prize and make it yours!"

(1 Cor 9:24 AMP)

Cooperation involves more than relationship. Of course, we must be in relationship with God and we come into relationship with Him the moment we receive Christ as our Saviour – this is our starting point. Relationship with the Lord is essential – it puts us in the running for our God-given destiny. Without making this decision for Christ, we do not qualify to participate in the eternal purpose God has for our lives. So, if you have not made this decision, I want to encourage you to pause here, take a moment and put yourself in the running (pray the short prayer on page 229).

Participation is necessary, but it is not yet the whole. Participation alone will not ensure that we finish or win this race. Something more is required from us if we are to achieve that.

Many years ago, I participated in a 10km running race. I was by no means a seasoned runner: jogging more aptly describes what I did a few times a week to keep fit, even if I do have perfect running feet! This is a running joke in our family (that one is for my husband, who loves his puns) and started after I visited a sport's podiatrist to ensure I was jogging in the right shoes. After completing his assessment, he declared that I had "perfect running feet" (the expert's words, not mine) and that I would be running marathons in no time. We all laughed about it together afterwards because the family knew that I lacked the running prowess to match said feet and that I wouldn't be entering any marathons! Anyhow, at the suggestion of a friend, we entered a 10km race together.

On the morning of the race, I was surprised to find that there were hundreds of participants. There were a few different distances to choose from, but all of us would start off and end in the same place. Some of the entrants really looked the part; they were serious runners, more the marathon type than the casual jogger type. They were already glistening with sweat (had they run there as a warm-up?) and I could tell by the different colour on their race numbers that they'd signed up for the marathon. These were the hard-core runners and their physical condition showed it.

We registered and then lined up for the start. We stood way back because a large throng of runners was bunched up ahead of us. The anticipation started building as the clock marked the countdown and then off we went. Initially, we could do nothing more than walk as we hung around waiting for those ahead to pull away, so we could get moving. This took a long time, but eventually we could start jogging as the walkers separated from the runners and the road opened up. I enjoyed the experience and even managed to cross the finish line, but I came nowhere near the race winners.

Having qualified for the race, I could enter, but I had no intention of winning. I trained, I participated and I finished, but I didn't win it. The effort I put into the race was not on the same level as the runner who went on to win it. The difference between the race winners and me was obvious.

Likewise, participating in our divine race of purpose doesn't necessarily mean we're running in a way that ensures we will win. It doesn't automatically result in us obtaining the prize of connecting our dots from beginning to end. Running our race to win this prize will require something far more than qualification (through Christ) and participation (in our ongoing relationship with Him). It requires a response that reaches beyond our basic participation with God to become a lifestyle of unrelenting cooperation with Him.

2. COOPERATION IS RELATIVE

"Then He said to them, "Pay attention to what you hear. By your own standard of measurement (that is, to the extent that you study spiritual truth and apply Godly wisdom) it will be measured to you (and you will be given even greater ability to respond) – and more will be given to you besides."

(Mark 4:24 AMP)

The act of cooperation is wholly relative. We tend to define the parameters of what cooperation with God will look like and it is usually in a way that suits us most. Come on, you know what I'm saying is true! We decide how far we'll go in our cooperation with the Lord based on what and when we're willing to do it. Does this sound like you? It certainly sounds like me!

When I wrote this chapter in 2020, the entire world was engaged in an unprecedented fight against Covid-19. In South Africa, we experienced a five-week national lockdown and were unable to leave our homes unless it was for essential food or medicine. The only businesses that were allowed to remain open were those that were considered essential services.

There were very detailed rules about what was and what wasn't allowed. President Cyril Ramaphosa even declared a national state of disaster and deployed the military to assist the police in ensuring that all citizens cooperated with the lockdown restrictions.

So how did we respond? A week into the lockdown, the local news showed police officers arresting a bridal couple who had gone ahead with their wedding day festivities despite the lockdown[3]. I watched this bride in her beautiful wedding dress being pushed into the back of a police car – not the way you want your wedding day to be! This was this couple's measure of cooperation with the lockdown restrictions.

From my verandah, I saw the occasional dog walker or jogger go by – both were clearly prohibited. Even a government minister broke the lockdown restrictions by going to lunch at a friend's house and then posted pictures of their forbidden celebration on social media[5].

Each of these demonstrated the levels of cooperation among South Africans. Some unashamedly broke the restriction rules and others stayed locked in their homes in compliance with all the regulations. So, the act of cooperation is relative because cooperation requires a personal response and we all respond in different ways and to different degrees.

Cooperation is something we personally give to God and we all give a different measure. We all respond differently. My measure is not the same as yours. There are a number of factors influencing our responses, but I believe they can be distilled down to the next two points.

3. COOPERATION IS ROOTED IN LORDSHIP

"Let all the house of Israel therefore know for certain that God has made him both Lord and Christ, this Jesus whom you crucified."

(Acts 2:36 ESV)

Cooperation is firmly rooted in lordship. Let me explain what I mean by this for those who might not be familiar with the term "lordship".

The word "Lord" in the above verse basically means "master"[6]. When we call Jesus Christ our Lord, we are stating that He is our Master; the One who rules over our lives. Consequently, we submit all of our lives to His lordship.

At the time of our salvation, we received not only a new start (2 Cor 5:17), but also a new Master – Jesus Christ (Gal 2:20). Choosing the former apart from the latter is not a Biblical option, for God has made Jesus *both* Lord and Saviour. Thus, as believers, we cannot seek to divide Jesus into two by holding Him as only our Saviour, but not our Lord.

The Bible makes it clear that salvation is not just about being born again. This is merely the starting point that ushers us into a brand-new life in Christ. From here, we are to live our new life according to our new identity and we do this by continually submitting our daily lives to the transforming work of His Spirit (Phil 2:12–13).

Accepting Jesus as the Lord of our lives means that we can't carry on living the way we did before our salvation, as Paul reminds us:

> Those who belong to Christ Jesus have crucified the flesh with its passions and desires (Gal 5:24 NIV).

Rather, with Jesus as our new Master, we vacate the throne of our lives and allow Him to lead us. This is a daily process and requires our ongoing decision to "throw ourselves wholeheartedly and full-time... into God's way of doing things" (Rom 6:13 MSG).

Lordship is a matter of obedience. Jesus addresses this directly when He says, "Why do you call me, 'Lord, Lord,' and do not do what I say?" (Luke 6:46 NIV). Calling Jesus our Lord (Master) means that we continually seek to obey His Word. And by obeying His Word, we allow the Holy Spirit to transform our lives, so that we gradually become more and more like Christ in every way: our actions, speech and responses (2 Cor 3:18; Rom 8:29).

Lordship is also synonymous with surrender. It is through lordship that we lay aside our ways and surrender to His, as we seek to obey His Word in fulfilling His will.

Now when it comes to cooperating with the Holy Spirit, this daily relationship of lordship is indispensable. We simply cannot work in cooperation with His Spirit when we don't habitually do what He tells us to do (Jas 1:22). Have you ever tried to direct someone who won't listen to your instructions? It's a task doomed to failure.

Without surrendering to His lordship, we simply have no basis for cooperation with the Holy Spirit. Without cooperation we are flying blind and ultimately choosing our own course. Connecting dots on our own means we might be on an entirely different page to the one He intended for us.

This is a very dangerous place for us to be in. It not only has a major impact on our dot journey, but it has major implications for how we're following and relating to Jesus as our Lord (Matt 7:21–23; Mark 10:17–31; Luke 14:25–35). The way we follow Jesus has eternal consequences (Matt 7:21-23). Therefore, it's imperative that we keep checking to ensure that we're responding to Jesus the way He wants us to. He has clearly outlined this for us in His Word.

The good news is that when we do fail in this (much the same way the original 12 disciples did), we can set it right with God in a moment. All it requires is a prayer of repentance:

> If we confess our sins, he is faithful and just to forgive us our sins and to cleanse us from all unrighteousness (1 John 1:9 ESV).

I encourage you to pause here to consider whether your current lifestyle indicates that Jesus is the Lord of your life. Take a moment to ask Him to put His finger on those areas in your life that haven't yet been submitted to Him. Ask Him to highlight where you might have stopped doing His will.

Then surrender them all to His lordship – even that one area you know He has been speaking to you about for a long time. Ask Him to help you respond in these areas with new acts of obedience.

The time to set this matter of lordship right is now, not tomorrow or next week. His loving arms of grace are waiting to receive you. You see, when we flounder in the area of lordship, we don't try harder – we surrender further. We yield more of our lives to Jesus, so that His Spirit can empower us to do the will of the Father:

> ...for it is God who works in you to will and to act in order to fulfil his good purpose (Phil 2:13 NIV).

We revere Jesus as Lord by His grace alone, not by our efforts. His grace enables us to respond to Him with whole-hearted devotion. His grace empowers us to do His will. His grace enables us to surrender our lives to His lordship. It is always a work of His grace and never a work of our own efforts (2 Cor 12:9; Rom 5:20).

We pave the way for cooperation with His Spirit by cultivating the daily discipline of continually surrendering our lives to His lordship.

4. COOPERATION MUST BE DEVELOPED

"... work out your own salvation with fear and trembling, for it is God who works in you, both to will and to work for his good pleasure."

(Phil 2:12-13 ESV)

Cooperating with God's purposes doesn't come naturally to us; it's not something we are born with. We don't roll out of bed in the morning and instinctively start cooperating with God. No, it's something we must learn and be intentional about developing every day.

We're the ones who connect our dots: it's our cooperation that's needed if God is to navigate us successfully through our lives. The Bible calls this individual responsibility the working out of our salvation (Phil 2:12).

We must recognise that cooperation with God is progressive. It's a work that is continually developing as we learn to heed His voice, grow in obedience and mature spiritually. But this progression is not something that happens organically: it requires ongoing effort and must be intentionally cultivated. This cooperation is like the mandatory team-building sessions I had to attend when I was still working in the corporate world.

These annual events were planned to foster collaboration between employees so that we'd be able to work together more productively. Whenever you have two or more people working towards the same objective, there has to be a team effort if the goal is to be realised. And the various organisations I've worked for invested lots of time and resources on team-building.

Working as a team requires effort and practice. It's no different when it comes to learning to work with the Holy Spirit.

Our teamwork is the substance of His lordship and its effectiveness is determined by the extent to which we are committed to keep progressing. This is perhaps the primary reason why we all give a different measure when it comes to our personal response of cooperating with Him.

As Christ followers, we're all in the same race, but we're certainly not all running in the same way. Some of us are simply walking or doing a casual walk-run. Others are jogging at a moderate pace. Some of us have given up and are sitting down at the side of the road, watching others pass them by. And then there are those that are running the race with focus: to win the prize.

Only we know which one of these scenarios applies to us. So, how are you running right now? Are you walking, jogging, running or sitting down? What scenario most accurately reflects your level of cooperation? If you're sitting, what has caused you to give up and abandon the race?

Considering all that is at stake, I encourage you not to rush through reflection, but instead really examine the way you are running this race of faith. You have been called to run it to obtain an eternal reward (1 Cor 9:24). This reward is our destiny fulfilled – all our dots joined in the right sequence and our eternal picture completed and revealed. This prize is worth winning, so let's spur each other on!

> *Do you not know that in a race all the runners run, but only one receives the prize? So run that you may obtain it. (1 Cor 9:24 ESV).*

Chapter 5:

COOPERATION DEMONSTRATED

"... your Teacher will not hide himself any more,
but your eyes shall see your Teacher.
And your ears shall hear a word behind you,
saying, "This is the way, walk in it,"
when you turn to the right or when you turn to the left."
(Isa 30:20-21 ESV)

The Holy Spirit, our great partner, inspired the writing of the Word of God. These Scriptures are given for our benefit to help us to walk in the fullness of Christ (2 Pet 1:20-21; 2 Tim 3:16). Within them we find a template for cooperation. The Bible is full of examples of men and women working in full cooperation with God as a pattern for believers to follow.

So, let's take a closer look at how two biblical characters ran their divine race and what the resulting impact was. Both of them exemplify cooperation with God, but the first serves as the epitome of working together with Him. His name, as you may have guessed, is Jesus of Nazareth. Now don't throw up your arms just yet! I know it's intimidating considering Jesus as a pattern to follow, but let me explain why it's not as difficult as you think.

During his life on earth, Jesus – the man – had to learn to live in obedience to God (Heb 5:8). As a matter of discipline, he too had to surrender his will and his ways to God (Phil 2:8). Jesus, through his human soul, had to discover the way to an intimate relationship with God. Jesus had to develop a daily routine of lordship by turning away from the things of this world and living for God – just as you and I must. He also had to continually prioritise God in everything. And he too had to commit to keep on growing in his relationship with God – just as we must. Fully human, Jesus of Nazareth had no advantage over us in this matter (Phil 2:8).

Beset with the same challenges we face on earth, this man did discover intimacy with God and relentlessly pursued Him. Through this single-minded pursuit of God, Jesus went on to master, through his daily routine and choices, full cooperation with the Holy Spirit. It was a daily discipline that translated into a lifestyle lived like this:

> So Jesus said to them, 'Truly, truly, I say to you, the Son can do nothing of his own accord, but only what he sees the Father doing. For whatever the Father does, that the Son does likewise' (John 5:19 ESV).

In the previous chapter, we considered the relative nature of cooperation and how it varies from person to person. Well, here we find a man on earth operating at its zenith. Jesus only did what he saw God doing. Think about what it takes, in the way of cooperation, to mimic someone's every move.

We can only imitate someone accurately when we make a close study of their ways. For example, consider how much time actors spend studying the character they're playing when preparing for a movie role. They know that the more time they can spend around the person observing the nuances of their mannerisms, the better they'll be able to emulate them.

For Jesus to imitate God to the degree that he did required no less effort. Jesus must have invested a tremendous amount of time in practising His relationship with God, observing everything about His character and ways in order to imitate His every detailed move. It signifies the closest of relationships, one rich in intimacy.

It was this ongoing daily effort on the part of Jesus that produced this high level of cooperation with Him. And as a result, Jesus, went on to realise his God-given destiny (John 17:4). As a human being, Jesus connected all his dots in sequence, from beginning to end with nothing missing. In doing so, he set the standard of cooperation. He demonstrates that it is entirely possible for a human being on earth to live a daily life in full and close cooperation with the Spirit.

Nonetheless, we remain thoroughly intimidated by His example. We find it difficult to imagine that we could accomplish the same level of intimacy with God because while we know that Jesus was completely human, we also know that he was the only begotten Son of God. Surely, this means he had some sort of edge over us, which in turn leads us to conclude that we could never reach the same level. But as intimidating as the example of Jesus may be, it does not change the facts. The man, Jesus of Nazareth, is the epitome of a lifestyle lived in full cooperation with God.

Let's move on to another example and look at the life of a man who was in *every way* just like us. He wasn't the begotten Son of God. He wasn't sinless. He was completely ordinary and his name is Samuel. He was the first-born son of Elkanah and Hannah, and we find his story in the first Book of Samuel.

As a young boy, Samuel is set apart by his parents to serve God and placed under the guidance of Eli the High Priest (1 Sam 2:11). This was done to fulfil a promise Hannah made when she cried out for God to give her a son (1 Sam 1:11). As we follow his training and ministry, we notice something quite remarkable about Samuel's relationship with God. First, he had a connection with God that was truly uncommon in his time and second, it was obvious to everyone. Israel repeatedly witnessed Samuel and God's amazing teamwork.

Over the 300[7] to 350[8] years that various judges governed over Israel, there had been a great falling away from the worship and ways of God (Judg 2:11–14; 18-19). As a result, the nation suffered great losses, both socially and spiritually (1 Sam 3:13; 4:10–11; 21–22). Juxtaposed against this bleak backdrop, we find the man Samuel whose love for and obedience to God, bolstered Israel's fortunes (1 Sam 2:35; 7:3).

In a time when the pursuit of the things of God was scarce in Israel, Samuel's life and ministry as a prophet were accompanied by many miracles. In response to Samuel's prayers on behalf of Israel, God supernaturally defeated the Philistine army and, on another occasion, miraculously sent rain out of season (1 Sam 7:10; 12:17). It was as if through the signs He performed, God wanted His people to take notice of what He had found in Samuel.

Everyone knew that Samuel had a direct line to God and was therefore not a man to be trifled with. In fact, when Samuel came into town, the elders became nervous as to why he was there. For the people of Israel, a meeting with Samuel represented a meeting with God (1 Sam 16:4).

What was it about him that set him apart? Samuel was not the only man in Israel that had a prayer life, he was not the only one that had access to God's laws and he was certainly not the only minister of God – there was an entire priesthood. What made him different from all the other prophets and priests in

Israel at that time? And what was the reason for his direct and very visible connection with Heaven?

A look into Samuel's life uncovers the answers. Throughout his ministry, we find a familiar interplay between God and Samuel. God issues him an instruction and Samuel's spontaneous response is obedience. In Samuel, God had found a reliable partner, a man who as a matter of routine worked together with Him towards His determined end. There is one simple statement in the Bible that summarises the entire governing theme of Samuel's life: "Samuel did what the Lord commanded" (1 Sam 16:4). This statement of obedience captures the fundamental nature of his relationship with God.

This sounds a lot like the statement Jesus made in John 5 about only doing what He saw His father do. Samuel was also a man bent on obedience to God and he too was a doer of the Lord's commandments. Like Jesus, Samuel is a remarkable demonstration of a man who fully orientated his daily life to cooperate with God's purposes – and the results were immeasurable.

One man working together with God impacted an entire nation and the course of human history. Israel's arch enemy (the Philistines) was subdued during Samuel's lifetime and as a result, they were able to recover vast amounts of lost territory (1 Sam 7:13–14). During his ministry, the Jewish nation experienced tremendous restoration and the way was made clear for God to bring even greater national advancement through the establishment of a kingdom and the rule of King David (1 Sam 11:14).

Samuel's obedience blessed an entire nation. His close cooperation with God impacted history and marked eternity.

But most importantly, he was an ordinary human being just like us. And if Samuel could do it, so can we.

Samuel is one of my favourite examples of cooperation. This was a man whose life from beginning to end exemplified full cooperation with God's purposes: what's more, he achieved this uncommon partnership under the Old Covenant. Samuel lived hundreds of years before the death and resurrection of Jesus Christ and before the Holy Spirit was poured out on all flesh on the day of Pentecost, yet this ordinary man managed to successfully order his daily life toward heaven. How much more are we able to do so today? Under the New Covenant, with the help of His indwelling Spirit, this is made even easier for us to realise (Heb 8:6).

Samuel is proof that we can orientate our daily life heavenward in full cooperation with God – even while we are on earth. His example firmly closes the door on all excuses we may try to find in response to God's call for our cooperation. His lifestyle sets a precedent that we are able to follow because of what Jesus has done for us through His death, resurrection and ascension. And Samuel is only one of many such examples. Throughout the Scriptures, the Lord has given us a clear demonstration of what a lifestyle of cooperation with Him looks like.

Remember that God is going to fulfil your destiny through *you*. Only Jesus could go to the cross to accomplish our redemption and only Samuel could transition the nation of Israel from the rule of judges to a kingdom. This was their respective destinies, their hidden picture to uncover. His plan for your life is brought to fruition through you alone – nobody else can live out your individual purpose.

So, when it comes to joining your dots, it is *your* cooperation that is required. And the level of cooperation you give Him determines the degree to which you will realise your God-given destiny.

The destination of the cross required Jesus' full cooperation. This doesn't mean that giving God His ongoing cooperation was always easy. On the eve of his crucifixion, Jesus invites us into one of his toughest moments of surrender. Here, as his human soul wrestled with the cross, we find Jesus praying to the Father in what I consider the most difficult, but also the most beautiful demonstration of His cooperation: "Father, if you are willing, remove this cup from me. Nevertheless, not my will, but yours, be done" (Luke 22:42 ESV). And when the Father did not remove the cup of the cross, Jesus, in full surrender, went willingly to it.

A lifestyle of cooperation is obvious throughout the life of both Jesus and Samuel. By it, they demonstrate for us that the act of cooperation is the very essence of discipleship. Cooperation should be our response to His call to follow Him (Matt 16:24). The moment we give our hearts to Jesus, we receive this call. As with any invitation, it necessitates a response. The invitation to follow God doesn't vary. In Christ, we all receive the exact same one.

The variation lies solely in our individual responses. The parable of the wedding feast highlights the importance of our personal response to His invitation (Matt 22). Here all the guests received the same invitation to the very same event, but it was their personal responses that led one to his farm, another to his business, some to commit crime and others to accept and attend the event.

Likewise, the way we choose to respond to the call to follow Christ matters a great deal to God because our response engages our destiny. Your cooperation is indispensable. By it, you connect with your destiny. So, when it comes to running your race to win the prize, all of heaven is depending upon your personal response of cooperation. How can we hope to connect the dots in our divine journey without this important teamwork?

Looking at the personal responses of both Jesus and Samuel, we find many corresponding truths we have already touched on. Both men learned obedience and modelled the principle of lordship. Both exhibited an unwavering routine of consecration as they orientated their lives heavenward in total surrender to God's purposes. As a result, both men went on to develop a lifestyle of cooperation and by it, both men fulfilled their God-given destiny. And likewise, so can you and I.

Chapter 6:

THE HABIT OF COOPERATION

"Morning by morning he awakens;
he awakens my ear to hear as those who are taught."
(Isaiah 50:4 ESV)

We have seen from both the life of Jesus and Samuel that the work of cooperation with God is more than just a decision – it is a discipline. Both men demonstrate a habit of ongoing cooperation.

Cultivating a lifestyle of ongoing cooperation with the Spirit requires a series of deliberate actions on our part, a set of spiritual practices that over time eventually become a matter of routine. There is simply no way to respond by the Spirit in a crisis unless we are well rehearsed in cooperating with Him beforehand.

Our arm of faith must know how to grab hold of the hand of partnership before the unexpected slams into our lives. This preparation needs to take place before the unexpected things happen.

Positioning ourselves as reliable partners means you might need to start doing some things differently. Perhaps you've already begun to recognise some of the changes you need to make. Maybe you need to put some new daily disciplines into your spiritual routine? Or perhaps you need to reorientate your discipleship heavenward, towards God's determined end, the way Samuel did? Regardless of what it is, we all need to make continual adjustments to our lives, particularly if our teamwork with God is to be effective.

It takes spiritual discipline to remain in a constant state of readiness before God. Only the spiritually fit can respond spontaneously, as Isaiah did: "Here I am. Send Me!" (Isa 6:8 NIV). Notice that I deliberately didn't say only the spiritually mature because no matter where we are in our spiritual development, we can all give God a response of obedience. We can pray, "Lord, I want to partner with You, but I don't know how, so please help me in this." This is a prayer of preparation; it's a prayer that asks to be introduced to the ways of cooperation with God and it's a prayer He will always answer.

Neither Jesus nor Samuel was born with an inclination towards spiritual preparedness. They both had to learn how to remain spiritually fit for God's use. The Bible tells us that Jesus had to learn how to be obedient to God:

> In the days of his flesh, Jesus offered up prayers and supplications, with loud cries and tears, to him who was able to save him from death, and he was heard because of his reverence. Although he was a son, he learned obedience through what he suffered (Heb 5:7–8 ESV).

Samuel also had to learn obedience. In 1 Samuel 3, we get a privileged glimpse into this spiritual training. Samuel slept in the temple, where the ark of God rested. The ark symbolised God's presence to the nation of Israel (1 Sam 3:4). One night, Samuel hears someone calling his name. Assuming it is the High Priest Eli, he runs to Eli's room and says, "Here I am, you called for me" (1 Sam 3:8 ESV). But Eli tells him that he didn't call for him. This happens twice before Eli realises that something greater is going on. Eli then teaches Samuel how to respond when God calls his name again. Samuel goes back to his bed and waits. "And the Lord came and stood, calling as at other times, 'Samuel! Samuel!' And Samuel said, 'Speak, for your servant hears'" (1 Sam 3:10 ESV).

I love the window God gives us into the intimate exchange between Him and Samuel in this tender training moment. It is a beautiful demonstration of just how important and personal our spiritual development is to God. The way God trains you and the means He uses may not be the same as the way He trained Samuel or the way He trains me, for we are all unique and called to do different things.

A large part of David's training took place in the fields of Bethlehem where, as a shepherd boy, he kept watch over his father's flocks. God used Peter's experience as a fisherman to prepare him for his future kingdom work as a fisher-of-men. Joseph's training ground was in slavery, overseeing his master's house. The list of varying scenarios goes on and on throughout the Scriptures.

When I compare my personal training script with other believers, it's also different. As a new believer, the Holy Spirit led me into spontaneous obedience through different types of fasting exercises. It basically translated into random invitations to practise delayed gratification. It started with small things like a packed treat in my lunchbox that I was really looking forward to at work. But when it came to eating it, the Spirit would gently nudge me with a thought like, "Delay it for an hour." I would then respond with obedience and do just that. Sometimes it would be a meal or a cup of coffee. At other times, it would be putting off watching TV to first go and spend some extra time reading the

Bible or praying. These gentle invitations of the Spirit became a daily part of my life.

Gradually, these calls for obedience came more frequently and began to stretch me even further. I remember one particular occasion. The Spirit had asked me to delay eating a chocolate for an hour, which I did. After the hour had passed, I was really looking forward to eating my well-earned bar of chocolate on my drive home from work. But just as I reached for it again, He spoke to me again with, "Can you delay it by one more hour?"

These invitations to practise giving Him spontaneous obedience happened so frequently that it didn't take me long to recognise that this was something God wanted me to be well versed in. I somehow knew, without knowing how, that practising obedience when I heard His gentle voice was an important lesson for me to learn. What began with delaying gratification by an hour eventually grew to waiting days or even weeks for what I wanted.

What I didn't realise was that I was being introduced to the Holy Spirit and was being trained to live a Spirit-controlled life. What did I know about that? I was only two years into my relationship with God and was quite clueless when it came to spiritual matters. And of course, it goes without saying that I failed many times in a number of these Spirit-led practice sessions.

But I did recognise that this was important to God, even though I didn't know how it was relevant in the greater scheme of things. This only became clearer much later as I matured as a Christian. Nevertheless, I was compelled by the Holy Spirit on these occasions and the fruit it has yielded in my life is the deep fellowship I now enjoy with Him.

I consider the Spirit's companionship the greatest gift I could ever receive. The thing I treasure most in this life is the privilege of hearing His quiet voice. My personal relationship with the Spirit is my greatest delight on this earth. I cherish Him.

I have lost count of how many times I have responded with blind obedience to something I have heard Him say to me. My husband and children can tell you many such stories, particularly the ones in which they were the involved. How many times did He nudge me in the middle of the night and say things like, "Go check on the kids" (who were all teenagers at the time)? I would wander sleepily down the stairs and always, without fail, find them doing something that they shouldn't have been doing. Back up the stairs I would march to fetch Stuart and he would always ask, "How did you know?"

"The Holy Spirit told me," I would reply.

But perhaps one of the earliest occasions is even more memorable because it saved my son's life. I was 23 years old and had been home a few days after giving birth to my second son, Tylan. He was eight days old. It was mid-morning and I had just finished feeding him and putting him to sleep.

With baby asleep, I got on with my chores and went outside to hang up a load of washing. Then I heard the gentlest voice, saying, "Check on Tylan right now." I had literally just left him minutes before. But in response to His voice, I immediately left the laundry to check on Tylan. When I got to him, he was blue from head to toe and not breathing. I picked him up and checked to see if there was anything blocking his airways – nothing.

I panicked. I considered running outside and screaming for help, but the only neighbour who was at home then was an elderly woman with emphysema who was permanently attached to an oxygen mask, so there was no help to be found there.

Terror-stricken, I realised it was up to me. I started shouting out to the Lord to help as I stood holding my blue, unconscious baby in my arms. I have never known such terror as the panic I experienced in that moment.

I wanted to weep hysterically and collapse in a heap on the floor, but instead I just stood there, crying out over and over again, "Jesus, help me! Lord, help me, please!" It took a few seconds before I heard His response. Even in the midst of my frenzied state, I heard it clearly, gentle but firm.

I felt a tremendous peace as I heard Him say, "You can do this – save him." I can't tell you how it happened, but the moment He spoke those words in my heart, it was as if someone flipped a switch in my brain and I went from sheer panic to absolute calm. A thought popped into my mind and I went into autopilot. I knelt down and laid Tylan on the bed, placing my mouth over his tiny nose and mouth. Gently, I began to blow air into his lungs.

An article had suddenly come to mind that I'd read years before when I was pregnant with my first son. It was about administering CPR to a baby. I remembered that I needed to place my mouth over both his nose and mouth and breathe very gently. I distinctly remembered the part about not breathing too hard because it can pop their little lungs.

I didn't pump his chest, I just repeated one breath after another. Between each breath, I prayed, "Help me, Lord. Save him!" I had just started this process when the telephone started ringing. We'd just installed a phone in our bedroom and I reached over from where I was kneeling to answer it. It was a timely call from my husband. Between breaths, I filled him in on the situation.

My husband's work was about a 20-minute drive from our house. While I waited for help, all I did was breath one soft breath after another into my baby boy without pause. I was so focused on breathing and praying, breathing and praying, that I hardly noticed that his colour had returned to a normal pink – it was no longer blue. At this point, I realised that he was getting oxygen, but he was still lying unconscious and motionless.

When my husband finally arrived, about 40 minutes had passed. Without missing a beat, I picked my baby up and continued to breathe into his lungs as I walked to the car and got in. As we drove full speed to the nearest hospital, I continued to breathe for him. Another 15 minutes passed and still my baby did not move.

When we arrived, the emergency staff were waiting for us as my mother-in-law had notified the hospital beforehand. Still breathing for him, I got out the car and walked up to them. A nurse grabbed Tylan out of my hands and rushed him to a special ward. This was the first time I'd let go of him since he'd stopped breathing.

The nurse placed Tylan on a bed and put a tiny oxygen mask on his face. As the oxygen started to flow, almost immediately, Tylan gained consciousness and started to cry. I hadn't shed one tear up till then. It was all I could do to concentrate on breathing and praying, breathing and praying for my baby boy. But when I heard him cry, I began to shake and weep uncontrollably. I was overwhelmed with what the Holy Spirit had done. He had helped me save my baby boy!

After stabilising him, the attending paediatrician and nurses commended me. "Well done," they said. "You saved his life by administering gentle breaths without pause." All I could do was praise God! I was in total awe of what He had done for me in that moment of sheer terror.

What if I hadn't been prepared beforehand to hear and respond to His gentle nudges? If He hadn't trained me in obedience, I wouldn't have been prepared for that crisis. The bottom line? Had I not heard Him and responded instantly that day, while outside hanging up the washing, my son would have died.

But I was ready to meet that unexpected event – and not because of something I had done or some spiritual level I had achieved, but only because I had yielded to the same voice many times before. I had no idea that I would encounter that situation in the future. I had no idea how to save my eight-day-old baby, but He did. All He needed from me in that moment of crisis was to let Him lead me through it, something He had been faithfully training me to do all along. How then can I not praise Him for His faithfulness and goodness in this regard!

At the time, I was unaware of the Lord's purpose. Thankfully, I didn't have an eating disorder. I knew that He wasn't exercising me in this particular way for any dietary benefit. I could very easily have dismissed His gentle nudges that seemed to pop up randomly and without obvious benefit. I had absolutely no idea that as I yielded, little by little, to His will, I was in effect preparing today for my tomorrows.

I'm nobody special or extraordinary – ask anyone who knows me. God doesn't have any favourites (despite what the bumper stickers say!) If He did it for me, He can do it for you. I was a young mother when this happened and I'd only been walking with God for two years. I didn't even have a grasp on all the basics of Christianity. Even today, decades later, I'm still an ordinary believer. And just like you, I must read my Bible and pray daily. I am that ordinary someone who must walk out her salvation by means of submitting to a daily relationship of lordship with Jesus.

We are ready to begin cooperating with God from the moment we receive Christ. All He needs from us is our response.

Likewise, God wants to prepare you for the unexpected things that are coming in your life. Even today, there is something He needs to train you in, so that you will be ready for your tomorrows and whatever they may bring. But in order for Him to do so, you must yield to Him today.

A word of caution: be wise in what you ascribe as belonging to the Holy Spirit. Don't go off beam and assign every voice you hear to God. The Bible tells us to test every spirit: "Beloved, do not believe every spirit, but test the spirits to see whether they are from God..." (1 John 4:1 ESV). And again, "But test everything; hold fast what is good. Abstain from every form of evil" (1 Thess 5:21-22 ESV).

If you're not sure, check it out with your pastoral leaders. Just the other day, I counselled a young woman who was convinced that God had led her into a fast of repentance for a sin she had repented of 10 years before. As I showed her some Scriptures, she could clearly see that this was not of God. But by the time she'd come to me, she'd already put herself through days of crushing condemnation. The Spirit of God will never contradict the Word of God (John 16:14). Go to your pastoral leaders for their help if you need it. And if your leaders are telling you to do things that contradict God's Word, then leave that church and find one that is teaching truth!

So how did my story with Tylan end? After he regained consciousness, the paediatrician admitted him to the neonatal ICU for monitoring. It was a traumatic few days, with tubes and wires coming out of every hole in his little body. I wasn't allowed to pick him up and hold him. I could only touch him through the holes on the sides of the incubator.

Finally, he was diagnosed with a lazy epiglottis or laryngomalacia. Apparently, it was his lazy epiglottis that had collapsed and blocked his airway the morning he stopped breathing and went blue. The evidence of his condition had been there from birth because he was a noisy breather, particularly when he was breastfeeding.

After the diagnosis, I was sent with Tylan by ambulance to see a specialist at another hospital. The surgeon told me that he needed to take my newborn into surgery and stitch his epiglottis to the back of his larynx to prevent future episodes. He also explained the dangers of surgery for newborns and rattled off a number of frightening risk factors. The risks were enormously high, and in warning me of these risks, he mentioned that Tylan could die on the operating table during surgery. The fog had not yet lifted; I was still navigating my way through it.

I sat holding Tylan, listening to the doctor, all the while quietly asking the Lord to show me what to do. Once again, a gentle voice spoke to my heart, "Don't do it. Trust Me: he is going to be fine." I had my answer. So, I got up and thanked the doctor for his time and expertise. I told him that I'd considered all he'd said and had decided that I wasn't going to risk my baby's life by doing the surgery at this stage. I will never forget the way he looked at me then. It was a mix of pity and disdain. He warned that by not doing the procedure, my baby could die and how would I feel about that? Again, I politely thanked him and left.

He was a specialist, a highly trained medical expert. I'm not taking anything away from his expertise or the importance of medical help when we need it. I was grateful for it – truly. I have heeded the medical advice of doctors more than I have not. But what that doctor didn't know was that three days earlier, God's gentle nudges had saved my baby's life. I trusted His voice then and I was sure as anything going to trust Him now.

Do I need to say it? My baby never stopped breathing like that again. Of course, I took all the necessary precautions. I wasn't negligent or naïve – the familiar voice of the Holy Spirit was leading me. Tylan slept next to my bed on a little pad that recorded his pulse; if he stopped breathing, an alarm would go off. I had the paediatric oxygen mask and oxygen supply and knew how to use it if I had to. I had done my homework and read up on a lazy epiglottis. I knew that this condition was something children often grow out of and I trusted God to heal my son. Nevertheless, I was committed to using whatever medical interventions were available to me and he went for regular paediatric check-ups as we monitored his condition.

His noisy breathing was ultimately a godsend and, in the end, it was the only sign I really needed. If I couldn't hear the noises he made as he slept, I knew to go check on him. I was a mother who didn't want a quiet baby – it was the last thing I hoped for! I needed him to be noisy all night long. It's how I knew he was still alive.

Again, I need to remind you to please use godly wisdom. Don't ignore medical advice – that is not what I was doing. I took all the medical precautions I needed in case Tylan stopped breathing again. The paediatric ICU staff trained me in this before we left the hospital. Don't listen to every voice in your head and ascribe it to God – this is also not what I did. If you haven't had tried-and-tested accounts of hearing God's voice, obeying Him and seeing the results yourself, then please don't make assumptions as to what is of God in serious situations. Rather make these significant decisions together with your spiritual leaders.

I also don't want you to make decisions for your own situation based on *my* personal walk with God and then blame God (or me) when it doesn't work out – this is extremely foolish. Use godly wisdom; there is much safety in the counsel of many, so surround yourself with these spiritual voices of maturity (Prov 15:22). I'm recounting my story not as a doctrine or faith formula, but to highlight the great value of developing a lifestyle of cooperation with the Holy Spirit.

Today, Tylan is 30 and married to his beautiful Julia. One of the sweetest moments I had with my son was when, at the age of 12, I again got the opportunity to tell him about God's amazing providence in his life.

We were back in hospital together. He was staying overnight for monitoring to see if all was well with that infamous lazy epiglottis. He was still a noisy sleeper and the paediatrician was concerned that he hadn't grown out of it yet.

Although I'd told him this story on numerous occasions, for some reason, with time on our hands, this time it really registered with him. I will never forget that poignant moment as I shared the way things had unfolded that morning. We both sat there with fresh tears in our eyes, deeply moved by the goodness of God in saving his life.

> *... he leads them and they follow because they are familiar with his voice (John 10:4 MSG).*

Chapter 7:

PERSONAL REFLECTION

"Whether you turn to the right or to the left,
your ears will hear a voice behind you,
saying, 'This is the way; walk in it.'"
(ISA 30:21 NIV)

Preparing our faith for the unexpected things requires our active partnership with the Holy Spirit. When it comes to the details of our personal lives, He is ready to lead us from one dot to the next, at the right time and in the right order. But if we are to realise all this great value in His help, we must give Him our response of unreserved cooperation.

Jesus of Nazareth is the epitome of cooperation. He modelled cooperation for us in both his personal teamwork with the Spirit and his relationship with His disciples. When Jesus chose and called His disciples, He lived and worked with them every day. They did life together. They ate together, went places together, worked together and were in constant conversation with each other.

By this, Jesus demonstrates the kind of relationship He has called us into. He wants to work with us the way He did with those 12 original disciples. Because He lives in us, by His indwelling Spirit, we can have this most intimate togetherness in active partnership with Him every day (1 Cor 3:16).

God didn't abandon us to navigate through the fog of the unexpected things alone; He gave us the handle of partnership. It is ours for the taking. And if we are, like Jesus and Samuel, to hear the voice of the Spirit, directing us with the words, "This is the way, walk in it" (Isa 30:21 NIV), then it must become a familiar and well-worn handle in our lives. It must be a handle our hand of faith can easily hold onto when a crisis hits.

So, let's act now! Let's familiarise our hand with the feel of this handle and begin practising effective partnership with God. Your partner, the precious Spirit of God, is waiting for your response.

Putting It Into practice: Handle of Partnership

Spiritual Insight: God needs my ongoing cooperation.

1. Read 1 Corinthians 2:9–16:

a) What kind of value do you think a partnership with the Holy Spirit will bring to your personal dot journey?
b) How would you rate your level of partnership with the Spirit right now? Choose a number between 1–10 (1 being not active at all and 10 representing fully engaged).
c) What one thing can you start doing today that will make you more active in your partnership with the Holy Spirit?

2: Read 1 Corinthians 9:24–27.

a) How are you running your personal race? Are you merely participating or running to win it?
b) Verse 27 highlights the importance of daily disciplines. What new daily discipline can you add to your spiritual routine today to ensure that you are not running aimlessly as Paul says?

3. How do the spiritual practices of both Jesus and Samuel challenge you?

b) What will you take away from their example and how will you begin implementing it in your personal life?

4. The Oxford dictionary defines cooperation as "*the process of working together to the same end*".

a) List three ways you are working together with God to achieve His purposes in your life.
b) Is there anything you may need to pause and repent about in this regard?

4. Read Luke 6:46–49.

a) The author wrote that, "Without lordship, you and I simply have no basis for cooperation with the Holy Spirit." From this story, which person best describes you? What are you currently building your life on?
b) What is the extent to which you have or haven't given Jesus lordship over your life?
c) List one area in your life that you know needs to be surrendered to Him. What do you need to do to make this decision to surrender? Pray with others as you ask God to help you.

5. Make a start today. Using the various aspects of cooperation covered in this chapter as a broad framework, carve out your own unique plan to increase your teamwork with Him.

The decision to make an effort is already a response of cooperation. Now determine to convert your decision into a daily discipline of regular and routine obedience.

SECTION 2:
HANDLE OF PERSPECTIVE

"Now faith is the assurance of things hoped for, the conviction of things not seen."
(Heb 11:1 ESV)

Holding firmly to the handle of partnership, our faith is perfectly positioned for the support of another important handle – the handle of perspective. Perspective is a powerful tool. It allows for a different interpretation of what is evident before us. And in the fog of the unexpected things, seeing beyond the obvious is crucial.

Perspective is directly and inextricably linked with our faith (Heb 11:1) and subsequently has a real impact on our cooperation with the Spirit. Our perspective determines what we can see and how we perceive things happening around us. This is so well illustrated in the way Vocabulary.com defines the word "perspective":

> *Perspective* has a Latin root meaning "look through" or "perceive", and all the meanings of *perspective* have something to do with looking. If you observe the world from a dog›s perspective, you see through the dog›s eyes.[9]

Our perspective frames our world and determines our perceptions. These perceptions inform our faith (Heb 11:1). As believers, our faith has two perspectives to choose from: either we view our situation through a natural lens, which leads to natural observations or we look through a spiritual lens, which leads to spiritual observations. The observations we make about our circumstances, particularly in times of crisis, are a direct result of the lenses we are looking through.

Our dominant perspective is obviously our natural one: it is the one we use the most in our seen world. It is our default lens, so to speak. But when it comes to our faith, we don't rely on our natural lens, as the opening scripture reveals. Faith resides in the *unknown*, in the things we hope for, even when we do not yet *see* them (Heb 11:1; 8). To have faith means that we believe in the promises of God without *seeing* the actual evidence of their fulfilment in our circumstances. The whole chapter of Hebrews 11 is dedicated to the theme of walking by faith, not by natural sight (2 Co 5:7). Our natural perspective is of little help to our faith when it comes to partnering with the Spirit through the fog-filled places of life.

Firstly, our natural lenses are woefully limited. While we are in this human body, we see only fragments of God's entire whole (1 Cor 13:9). With this restricted perspective comes a limited capacity to comprehend the vastness of God's eternal purposes. His mysterious ways are so much higher than ours (Isa 55:8-9). There are many things in our known world that we don't yet fully understand, never mind when it comes to understanding the things of God. He is omnipotent (all powerful) (Ps 147:5; 1 Jo 3:20), omnipresent (present everywhere at the same time) (Jer 23:24; Col 1:17) and omniscient (all-knowing) (Rom 11:33-36; Isa 46:10). We, on the other hand, are confined to our mere humanity (Jas 4:14).

Secondly, our natural lens is one that continually prioritises the seen over the unseen. We are well versed in searching for answers to our difficult circumstances within the familiar framework of the seen things, in our *known* world. As a result, we have an innate tendency to oversimplify things. We find familiarity in clear-cut solutions and so prefer black-and-white judgements to more nuanced observations: it is or it isn't; it's over here or over there; it's up or it's down. We don't do life in the vast span of greys that invariably hold the many mysteries of the unknown and complex ways of God. We *prefer* filtering things through our known world and our understood framework when forming conclusions.

When we meet with the unexpected things, our limited perspective poses a great threat to our faith and our ongoing cooperation with God. Our crushing circumstances loom large and loud, screaming for immediate answers and our automatic response is the one that is most familiar to us – our take on things. This is where we tend to seek answers, even when we must use our imagination to dream up weird notions about what has befallen others or us and why.

Our natural inclination in this regard is well demonstrated in the narrative of Job and his three well-meaning friends, Eliphaz, Bildad and Zophar. In the story of Job, disaster strikes and he is beset with a number of devastating circumstances. His friends come to support Job and offer to help him understand the reason for his suffering[10]. Theorising through their human limitations (1 Cor 13:9), they offer opinions as to why Job has met with these unexpected things. For these three friends, the diagnosis is simple: Job must have done something horribly wrong to bring all this misfortune on himself. Based on this assumption, they advise him to repent and plead for God's mercy in the hope that things might improve. How quick we are to whip out the rod of condemnation when the unexpected things happen (Rom 8:1)! We are so ready to beat others (and ourselves) with it as we surmise using our intellect and limited understanding.

If you are not familiar with the story of Job, I encourage you to read the book. It offers great insight into our natural inclination to judge others and the harm we can inflict when we filter the unknown things through the restriction of our human understanding. At one point, Zophar expresses just how woefully limited our natural perspective is when he says:

> Can you find out the deep things of God? Can you find out the limit of the Almighty? It is higher than heaven – what can you do? Deeper than Sheol – what can you know? Its measure is longer than the earth and broader than the sea (Job 11:7–9 ESV).

Ironically, Zophar can't stop himself from theorising the cause of Job's misfortune. But the benefit of Scripture gives us a very different perspective on Job's troubles. We are given a window into the unseen, spiritual world – and here we see a very different picture. Through the lens of the Spirit, we find something mysterious playing out in the spiritual realm, an intense war for Job's soul. His friends are wrong: his unexpected circumstances have absolutely nothing to do with any personal sin or wrongdoing (Job 1,2).

Oh, the folly of our human observation! God's response to Job in chapters 38 to 42 underscore the insufficiency of human understanding in the light of God's greatness[9]. Yet we are naturally driven by this insatiable appetite to make assumptions and ascribe labels to things, even when we don't know what that label should be. And herein lies the challenge of interpreting the unexpected things without relying on Spirit-inspired wisdom: we can get it horribly wrong. To the detriment of our faith and trust in a loving God. These assumptions often weaken our faith in a loving God, rather than fortifying it. Like Job, we are easily persuaded to blame God for what is happening to us (Job 9:22–23;10:2;27:2).

The issue of perspective remains an ongoing challenge in our walk of faith. We must continually choose to see the goodness and promises of God through the eyes of our faith, rather than our natural circumstances. This exchange of lenses is one we must regularly practise if we are to trust God in all things through faith (Heb 11). I love how the Holy Spirit patiently trains us in this exchange. We see it so beautifully in the lessons he taught the prophet Jeremiah.

Right at the beginning when he was called, we find Jeremiah in the School of the Spirit being taught to see with his eyes of faith, rather than his natural eyes:

> And the word of the Lord came to me, saying, "Jeremiah, what do you see?" And I said, "I see an almond branch." Then the Lord said to me, "You have seen well, for I am watching over my word to perform it." The word of the Lord came to me a second time, saying, "What do you see?" And I said, "I see a boiling pot, facing away from the north" (Jer 1:11–13 ESV).

I love the tenderness of this patient exchange as God teaches Jeremiah to engage his spiritual senses to interpret what will take place in the future. Now Jeremiah didn't actually see a physical almond branch or a boiling pot before him. He saw these images with his spiritual eyes. Here we find God sharpening Jeremiah's spiritual sight for His divine purposes. And Jeremiah wasn't the only one who received this type of training; Amos (7:8), Zechariah (4:1–8), Ezekiel (2:1–3), Daniel (7:1), John (Rev 4) and scores of others were patiently trained by the Spirit to activate their spiritual senses.

Today, we are also in the School of the Spirit. One of the primary reasons we were given the gift of the indwelling Holy Spirit is so that He could facilitate our spiritual learning and help us understand spiritual things. We need His ongoing help with this because, "The natural person does not accept the things of the Spirit of God, for they are folly to him, and he is not able to understand them because they are spiritually discerned" (1 Cor 2:14 ESV).

Spiritual things must be spiritually perceived (1 Cor 2:14). Spiritual things reside in the unseen, spiritual world: in order for us to access them, we must, by way of the Spirit, activate our spiritual senses, not our natural senses. Like Jeremiah, we too are being trained by the Spirit to activate, engage and develop the use of our spiritual senses because without them, it's quite impossible to know spiritual things.

Switching over to a spiritual perspective becomes critical when we meet the unexpected things. Without it, we see only natural things and make only natural deductions. Without it, our faith is unable to accurately interpret our circumstances within the bigger picture of God's sovereign purposes. And if our faith can't look through our crushing circumstances to behold the sovereignty and goodness of God, it will drown in unbelief and mistrust.

Mistrust and unbelief are a lethal combination; together they equal the proverbial pin that will pop our faith balloon (Heb 11:6). If we lose our faith in the midst of the chaos of our crisis, how can we hope to stay in partnership with Him when we need it the most? How can we navigate the dense fog without Him?

Our perspective defines the way we perceive our surroundings, as well as the way we navigate our way through them. Our perspective has a profound impact on our faith – either negatively or positively. Depending on the lens we use, we will either be actively strengthening our faith or weakening it. The one is a *faith-building perspective* and the other a *faith-eroding perspective.*

Chapter 8:

THE FAITH-ERODING PERSPECTIVE

A faith-eroding perspective will hinder our cooperation with God. It's a lens that forces us to view the unanticipated events of life through the limited perspective of our known world. This viewpoint calls our attention to natural, worldly things and places emphasis only on what we can see and understand about our current reality.

This is the lens Satan wants us to use when we meet the unexpected things in life. His goal is to get us to assess our circumstances by what is obvious before us – nothing more. And this is the perspective he will place before our eyes of faith at every given opportunity.

The devil has deliberately designed the faith-eroding lens to skew and tarnish the true image of God. Through this lens, God is conveniently labelled as the author of all suffering, devastation and loss. No matter what has befallen us or our loved ones, this lens firmly lays the blame with God. This lens purposefully obscures truth, so it really doesn't matter which argument he uses, all of them lead to the same perversion – blame God.

These arguments can take a variety of forms: God is harsh and unreliable, so He can't be trusted. Or God doesn't seem to care that much about people because just look at all the suffering on earth. Besides, if God is such a good, all-powerful God, then why doesn't He just put an end to it all or even better, why didn't He just prevent this from happening to you in the first place?

After all, you are a believer; you are a child of God; you spend all that time praying, reading the Bible and attending church, so why did God not avert this disaster on your behalf? And there are many, many more lies our enemy uses.

Satan is a truth twister (John 8:44). He has many truth-obscuring perspectives in his wicked arsenal and is an expert at using them. They are consistent with the persuasions he used at the very beginning, when he convinced Eve to see the forbidden tree through a different lens – one other than God's (Gen 3:2–7). The moment Eve looked at it, Satan sold her the package deal and we know the rest as she succumbed to his crafty deception. The enemy's onslaught was intended to prevent Adam and Eve from continuing in their walk with God to achieve His purposes. The ultimate intention was to break their cooperation with God. By using a different perspective, he succeeded. Adam and Eve fell out of cooperation with God.

The devil's tactics haven't changed. This remains Satan's strategy against God's people to this day. He wants to keep you and I from walking with God in His plans and purposes, and above all, he wants to break our ongoing cooperation with the Holy Spirit. Our cooperation with the Spirit works to displace Satan's power and authority on the earth (John 1:5; 8:12; Mal 4:2). We see the truth of this demonstrated in the lives of both Samuel and Jesus. Those in partnership with God are an immediate threat to Satan's wicked schemes and he will seek every opportunity to disturb, hinder or break our ongoing cooperation with the Holy Spirit.

The unexpected things present him with just such an opportunity. These traumatic places quickly expose our vulnerabilities, as our faith attempts to navigate us through the unpredictability of the unknown. Taken off guard, we search for quick solutions and it's at precisely this moment that the devil will offer us a faith-eroding lens to view our situation through.

When adversity strikes, Satan has his "God has let you down" speech ready. He will always make it personal and will offer up skewed reasons as to why you should hold a grudge against God. Before we exempt ourselves from this behaviour, we'd do well to remember that even Job, a man God esteemed for his righteousness (Job 1:8), succumbed to this tendency and blamed God for his unfortunate circumstances (Job 9:17–18). Like Job, many of us easily give in to these compelling falsehoods in the face of the unexpected things. Just think back to the last time you felt as if the Lord had let you down in some way and were tempted to withdraw from Him.

The faith-eroding lens has been expertly crafted to enlarge the size of our circumstances, while diminishing the size of our God. It supersizes our problems and places God far off in the distance, completely disconnected from what we are going through. How can we hope to go on with a partner we believe is no longer there and no longer cares?

The moment we put on this lens and accept the many lies that skew God's image, we let go of the hand of the Spirit and pause our working together with Him. Or worse, we might even push Him away and in so doing, grieve Him – the very One who longs to help us in our suffering.

Make no mistake, the god of this world is a cunning foe and a master deceiver; we do well not to underestimate his skill when it comes to hindering our ongoing cooperation with God (Jn 8:44). He will seize the opportunity of our crisis and our vulnerability to present us with many substitute perspectives as to why we shouldn't trust God. And he won't run out of persuasive arguments in this regard, for he has been in the lying business way longer than we've been in the truth business! It's therefore imperative that we remain wise and vigilant, so that we are not "outwitted by Satan" or left "ignorant of his designs" (2 Co 2:11 ESV).

Whose Calling Card Is It?

In the past, when people popped by for a visit and found nobody at home, they would leave a calling card behind. A calling card was usually personalised: it revealed the identity of the caller and announced their unexpected visit.

If we are to avoid the faith-eroding tactics of the enemy, we must learn to identify whose name is on the calling card of our circumstances. To help us, the Lord gives us a simple, but very effective strategy in Matthew 7:

> Beware of false prophets, who come to you in sheep's clothing, but inwardly are ravenous wolves. *You will recognise them by their fruits.* Are grapes gathered from thornbushes or figs from thistles? So, every healthy tree bears good fruit, but the diseased tree bears bad fruit. A healthy tree cannot bear bad fruit, nor can a diseased tree bear good fruit. Every tree that does not bear good fruit is cut down and thrown into the fire. *Thus you will recognise them by their fruits* (Matt 7:15–20 ESV).

The Lord's concern is that we will be duped into believing that something is true when it is actually false (i.e. false prophets) and as a result be misled (v. 15). Notice that the Lord warns us of the danger of face-value assumptions: it will look like a sheep because it will be dressed as a sheep, but this is nothing but a façade because it's really a wolf. He then goes on to give us a way to see past these initial sheep façades of falsehood by using discernment. Instead of looking at the obvious (the sheep) to determine its identity, the Lord directs our attention to what the subject before us is producing. He teaches us that something can only produce after its own kind (vv.16–18) and that if we learn to determine what something is producing, we're better able to identify it (v. 20). Jesus tells us that the fruit reveals everything!

The Lord's warning is clear – things are not always as they seem. There are times when we could mistake a dangerous wolf for an innocent sheep, when we could accredit something to God when it is indeed a camouflaged work of his enemy.

The strategy the Lord give us for recognising false prophets can also help us with the unexpected things. For the sake of our faith, we must look past the façade of our circumstances to see what is being produced: death, disease, divorce, hatred, destruction, fear or conflict. In this way, the fruit of our circumstances functions a bit like a calling card – they reveal who or what has dropped by. By learning to recognise the fruit of the unexpected things, we are in a better position to avoid the faith-eroding lens that so often cripples our faith and breaks our cooperation with God.

The Lord kept his lesson on discerning false prophets simple on purpose; the enemy is a master deceiver. Paul says that he even "disguises himself as an angel of light" (2 Cor 11:14 ESV). There are many opportunities for confusion when we meet the unexpected things, many competing perspectives to view our situation through. But every one of us can see what type of fruit a tree is producing. We might not all be able to tell a wolf from a sheep, the resemblance may be too close in appearance, but we can all see what fruit a tree is producing. Does it bear good fruit or evil fruit?

Satan presents the unexpected things in the guise of some form of "blame God". We do well to look at what the event is producing and resolutely reject the enemy's lie.

Loss, Devastation and Destruction are the Calling Card of God's Enemy

> The thief comes only to *steal* and *kill* and *destroy*. I came that they may have life and have it abundantly (John 10:10 ESV).

Satan is evil and therefore can only produce evil fruit. When we experience loss, destruction or death of any kind, this is the work of Satan. His wicked name is on that calling card. Don't fall for his lies as he tries to attach God's precious name to it: these evil deeds belong to him.

> God is light, and in him is no darkness at all (1 John 1:5 ESV).

> Every good gift and every perfect gift is from above, coming down from the Father of heavenly lights, who does not change like shifting shadows (Jas 1:17 NIV).

Don't entertain those thoughts that God is somehow to blame for your situation. It's not as if God was hosting some cosmic tea party when this happened to you and so, oops! Sorry... He dropped the proverbial ball on you. Don't accept the multitude of deceptions the devil wants to feed into your mind as to why God has suddenly begun producing loss, devastation and destruction. These tactics work to place our much-needed faith in a loving Father on shaky ground and this is exactly what the devil wants to achieve in your crisis.

Satan wants to drive a wedge between you and God; he wants to create uncertainty and doubt, cutting off your cooperation with the Holy Spirit. Remember that while God doesn't keep a record of your sins (Isa 43:25; Heb 10:15–18), Satan most certainly does and will regularly remind us of them and use them strategically against us. He fights dirty and keeps it personal. I could fill pages with the many lies that Satan feeds into our thought life, but in the end, they all have the same objective – to erode our faith in God (by twisting His true image) and to break our cooperation with His precious Spirit.

We recognise these lies by the fact that they always implicate God as the source of our woes. These lies may start off as subtle suggestions, but when we take them in, they quickly develop into doubt that erodes our faith (Matt 14:30; Luke 24:37–39). This leads us to blame God: His name is on the calling card of this tough situation.

Satan wants us to believe that God is responsible for loss, devastation and destruction; he will even give you Scriptures to prove it. This is not a new tactic; God's foe has long been twisting Scriptures to lead us astray (Matt 4:1–11). On these occasions, the image we have of God becomes critical. Thankfully, we have Jesus Christ as our template for who God is (John 14:7; 9).

Interpreting the Scriptures with a Christ-centred approach is a safeguard. With this practise, we can avoid assigning characteristics to God that are far from His true nature (John 14:6–7; 8–9). By keeping the person of Jesus before us continually, we can avoid signing God's name to works that are not His.

God Is Always Good

> Oh give thanks to the Lord, for he is good, for his steadfast love endures forever! (Ps 107:1 ESV)

God is good and can only produce good fruit (Eph 5:9). We find no evidence of pain, suffering and devastation in the Garden of Eden before the fall of Adam and Eve. These only entered the world after the fall as the consequences of sin (Gen 1–2).

We also have an accurate demonstration of the true nature and image of God in the person of Jesus Christ. This Jesus lens reveals the unending love and goodness of God. Jesus went out of His way to deliver the oppressed and heal those who were suffering. Jesus left His heavenly dwelling, came down to earth and became a man, so that He could die a criminal's death on a cross in our place (Phil 2:5–8). We behold the great love of God as He took the weight of the world's sin on Himself, so that we could be freed from sin's eternal death penalty (John 3:15–16). In everything Jesus did and said, the truth of God's goodness is fully revealed and by His works, we see that God is good and full of love (Ps 107:1).

God came to give us life and life abundantly (John 10:10). He didn't come to steal, kill and destroy – this is the work of Satan. If our faith is to remain steady through the many unknowns of the unexpected things, we will need to hold tightly to this truth. The very worst thing we can do is allow doubt to obscure God's image and separate us from His loving help.

Through social media, we have easy access to numerous narratives, making it even easier for Satan to peddle his substitute lies. We must become more vigilant in filtering everything we watch and hear through the life of Jesus, so that we can grow in the practice of spiritual discernment and ascribe the right works to the right source. The strength and stability of our faith depends on it. Likewise, our uninterrupted cooperation with His Spirit.

We test the veracity of the lenses we are viewing our circumstances through by looking at the fruit around us and asking, “Whose name is on this calling card?”

Chapter 9:

THE FAITH-BUILDING PERSPECTIVE

"I saw the Lord sitting upon a throne, high and lifted
up; and the train of his robe filled the temple.
Above him stood the seraphim.
Each had six wings: with two he covered his face,
and with two he covered his feet, and with two he flew.
And one called to another and said:
"Holy, holy, holy is the LORD of hosts;
the whole earth is full of his glory!""

(Isaiah 6:1–3 ESV)

A faith-building perspective is one that seeks to view the unexpected things through the eyes of heaven. This is a lens that affords us an eternal perspective, revealing a much bigger picture than the scenes playing out in our present reality (Is 55:8–9).

It's a lens that lifts our eyes of faith heavenward and fixes them firmly on a God whose ways are infinitely higher and better than human wisdom and understanding. It's a viewpoint that enables us to peer through the fog of our crisis and behold our sovereign God, seated on His throne, reigning in supreme authority over our lives as His covenant children.

Here our faith finds the solid ground it needs for ongoing cooperation with the Spirit because here we are again reminded that on this side of eternity, we can only ever see and know in part – never in full (1 Cor 3:12). So, instead of trying to fathom the unfathomable (like Job's friends), we allow our partnership with the Holy Spirit to shape our faith into an ever-increasing attitude of trust in God. We learn to trust in God's character, to cling to His goodness and faithfulness. We trust in His unfailing love. We trust explicitly in the person of Jesus Christ.

In this place of recognition and trust, we can let go of the spiritual gymnastics, the temptation to come up with the reasons for the unexpected things and instead find a much-needed respite in the knowledge that God is still in charge, despite what may be happening in our lives.

Through the eyes of heaven, we see that God is not restlessly pacing up and down before the throne, chewing on His nails, wondering what to do about our predicament. Rather, like Isaiah, we see the One who holds supreme authority over all things, both in heaven and on earth, *seated* on His throne (Isa 6:1). Nothing can take God by surprise and nothing can unsettle His sovereignty. We realise that our faith too can be safely *seated* in Him (Eph 2:6).

Unlike God, the unexpected things take us by surprise and unsettle our lives. In these places, it's difficult to think, never mind think clearly about which lens we are wearing. This is why we must prepare our faith ahead of time, before we meet the unexpected things. If we are to have any hope of overcoming through crises tomorrow, we must develop a faith-building perspective today.

A faith-building perspective leads our souls into an uncanny peace, much like the supernatural peace Jesus had when He slept through a raging storm (Mat 8:23–27). Despite the pounding waves and raging wind, there Jesus was – fast asleep. Can you picture the scene? The narrator tells us that the disciples, who were in the boat with Him, in the very same storm, were beside themselves with fear and believed they would all die. And there is Jesus, sleeping through it all!

This tells us one thing for sure – Jesus and His disciples had two very different perspectives on their surrounding circumstances and subsequently had two very different reactions to them. These contrasting responses give us further insight into the power of perspective and its effects on our faith.

Jesus slept through a storm that terrified His disciples. In an earlier chapter, we considered Jesus of Nazareth as the epitome of cooperation and citing John 5:19, we noted that Jesus only ever did what He saw the Father doing. Jesus took His cue from God. To understand the Lord's extraordinary response, we must follow His gaze heavenward – to the Father, upon whom His eyes were permanently fixed. What Jesus saw there, what He found in God, gave Him perfect rest and so, He slept.

In stark contrast, the disciples were in a panic and fearing for their lives. We can see by the details the eyewitnesses give, in describing the account, that the disciples were focused on the storm that had suddenly engulfed them. They saw howling winds and watched in terror as every crashing wave filled their boat with more seawater (Luke 8:23). What the disciples fixed their gaze to, the surrounding circumstances, moved them into panic and it crippled their faith. We know this because when in terror they wake Jesus, He connects their response of fear directly to their lack of faith: "Why are you afraid, O you of little faith?" (Mat 8:26 ESV). Eish* – those faith-eroding lenses we are so drawn towards!

---

* South African exclamation derived from Xhosa which is used to mean just about anything.

Notice that Jesus did not begin to spell out the "whys" of the storm. This information was clearly not a prerequisite to responding in faith because Jesus doesn't even go there. This is tremendously liberating; we don't need to know all the information about our unexpected circumstances to give God a response of faith in the midst of it. We don't need all the "whys" and "who's" answered to stay in cooperation with Him. We just need quiet trust in our Saviour.

This story is a lesson of faith. By it, we understand that if we are to perceive the unexpected things through the eyes of faith, we must learn to look beyond the obvious – beyond the storm – heavenward. We must search for God's view of the storm we're in.

To find this view, we fix our gaze firmly on the risen Christ. We look at Jesus Christ, seated at the right hand of the Father, ruling and reigning on the throne (Col 3:1; Heb 1:8). We build our faith looking to the One who is the cornerstone and very foundation of it, the One who is our hope and victory (Acts 4:11; 1 Pet 2:6; 1 Cor 3:11). We erode our faith by watching the wind and waves of our situation. The winds and waves obscure our view of Christ's victory and presence. The Saviour was right there in the sinking boat with the disciples, but this paled into insignificance at the sight of the raging storm. The Saviour, the One who saves us, is right there in the unexpected things with us, but if we focus only on the apparent threats, we will be unaware of His presence.

The struggle to give a response of faith rather than fear is very real, especially in the midst of a raging storm when our boat is being violently tossed by the waves of life. This I know personally.

My marriage to my first husband eventually ended. Coming to this decision was never easy; it was a long road and lasted many years, fraught with tremendous emotional upheaval. Years later, though, the Lord brought a wonderful godly man and his three children into my life. Having lived through many years of stormy waters, I was looking forward to some calmer seas – hoping for some plain sailing, so to speak.

Both Stuart and I had been married before and had our own children. Both of us had been through some significant soul trauma in our previous marriages. So, we knew that forging a new relationship, with all of these dynamics at play, wouldn't be easy. It was complex; we had to get to know each other with five children, all aged eight and under, in tow. We knew that bringing our two families together would be a challenge. On our first date as a couple, we went to the movies to see *Inspector Gadget*! Stuart sat on one end of the row with me on the other and sitting in between us were five little bodies! It would not be your normal courtship, this I knew, but at that stage I was unaware of just how turbulent these waters would turn out to be.

Without going into the details of my husband's story, I can tell you that his ex-wife had hurt him a lot. He is a one-woman guy, the kind of man that marries for life, so when his marriage ended, it wounded him deeply. He would say it smashed his heart completely and having watched his journey to restoration, I would agree. But before I go on, I must first contextualise it by sharing a dream the Lord gave me about three months before I met Stuart.

In this dream, I was breastfeeding three new babies: two boys and one girl. I woke up after this dream in the middle of the night, knowing it was profound and full of meaning. I got up and wrote the details of the dream in my journal and spent time in prayer, committing to nurture whatever He was bringing into my life. I prayed, "Lord, I receive these gifts from you. I will love and nurture them as a mother would her own children." In my heart, I imagined that these three babies symbolised something else: spiritual gifts or ministry assignments perhaps. I never for one moment imagined that the dream could be literal in meaning. That is, until I met Stuart on a school field one Saturday morning and he introduced me to his three children: two boys and a girl! Really, Lord, now You drop the symbolism? Had I known the dream was literal, I might not have so readily said yes!

Our relationship progressed prayerfully, as together we sought God for His will and His help. One evening, after visiting him and the children, as I was reversing my car out of Stuart's driveway, I heard the Spirit's gentle voice in my heart say, "We have taken a turn down a rough and bumpy road, but I am in this and will bring you through it, so hold onto Me and don't let go." Perhaps the fact that I was in reverse down a long and narrow driveway as He whispered these words should have clued me in to what lay ahead, but at the time the meaning escaped me entirely!

A year later, Stuart proposed. We celebrated our engagement by taking the kids out for milkshakes (I told you, not a normal courtship at all). The day after, we went to a friend's wedding and had a wonderful time together, but the very next morning, the unexpected happened. I received a distressed call from Stuart to say that he had been tormented by fear all night and that he was truly sorry, but he couldn't go ahead and marry me. The engagement was off. We had indeed taken a turn down a rough and bumpy road! In hindsight, I recognise the symbolism of the car's reverse gear.

I went straight to God. "What now, Lord?" was my prayer. "Do I stay and wait? Or is this not the relationship you have for me and I must go?" Each time I prayed, the Lord's reply was the same: "Stay, wait, I am working."

Stuart's marriage proposal had triggered the deep-seated wound of betrayal and it unleashed a tidal wave of fear that completely overwhelmed him. In that place of pain, he saw no other way out except to call it off. Not a great situation for either of us to be in, for sure, but I struggled to keep my eyes of faith on His promises and not on my jilted circumstances. Thankfully, I had many confirmations from the Lord that this was the man He had brought into my life, too many to list here. He had already forewarned me that things were going to get rough and told me to hold on because He was in it. I recognised His precious, gentle voice and I knew that He was absolutely trustworthy in all things, but the waves and wind thundered and the voice of the enemy declared: "Run from this relationship – run as fast and as far as you can!"

Stuart was already in professional counselling to work through his marriage trauma. Eventually, by the grace of God, we managed to salvage our relationship, pick up the pieces and keep moving towards marriage. We continued courting for a few more months and things kept improving as God's healing restored his soul and our relationship. A while later, Stuart proposed again – again, I accepted. This time we made it past 48 hours! We started planning our lives together as a blended family; we bought a house together, one that would be big enough for our new family of seven. Stuart sold his house and I gave notice on my apartment as we prepared for our upcoming wedding. We were planning to marry at the end of November, just as all the transfers took place so that we could all move into our new home together. We were excited for our new beginning.

It was the beginning of November and I was packing up my stuff in boxes for the imminent move at month-end. On 1 December, my sons and I would be moving into our new house with our new family – until we weren't. Yet again, fear raised its ugly head in Stuart's bruised soul and he called off the wedding. He was in torment and at the time, he saw no other way out, but to remove the trigger – our upcoming marriage.

Again, I went before the Lord and prayed the same prayer. "What now, Lord?" There was now a lot more skin in this game: we had bought a house together, I had given notice on my apartment and my children and I were packing boxes and had nowhere to go at month-end. Things did not look very promising at all. But again, I sensed the Lord clearly saying, "Stay, wait and keep trusting Me." This wasn't an easy thing for me to do! The sound of the waves and wind were now amplified and the urge to form my own conclusions about my circumstances and act on them was incredibly powerful. The temptation to look at my circumstances with my natural eyes tugged at my faith. I could feel the pressure of a crushing hand, throttling my attitude of faith and trust. The writing was on the wall: it was plain for all to see (our friends really did see it). This relationship was obviously bust, so I should just move on.

But… I had been introduced to the person of the Holy Spirit. I knew and trusted His voice. His still, small voice had saved my baby's life and He been so faithful in directing my steps to this point. I was determined not to stop trusting in Him now, even when giving up on this crazy relationship with Stuart seemed the rational thing to. Maybe I hadn't heard God properly? Maybe the dream didn't mean this? Maybe I had lost the plot completely, hoping against hope? Crazy thoughts like this warred against my continued cooperation with God. It was a mess, my heart was broken, my boxes were packed and I didn't know where my sons and I would be living come month-end. I was in a real predicament; my boat was most certainly sinking with every crushing wave of my unpredictable reality.

By His unfailing grace and with His help alone, I somehow managed to keep my eyes of faith fixed on what I did know. And I knew, beyond all shadow of doubt, that this had not taken God by surprise, even though it did me. God was still firmly seated on His throne. And somewhere in the deepest part of my soul, I knew that if I just kept my eyes on His sovereignty, that if I kept my faith hooked onto what I *did know* for sure, that He would somehow bring me through the fog of all these unknowns. As I did this, the most remarkable thing happened: a profound reassurance settled in my heart. I knew that despite all the unknowns, He would take care of me. I knew that my sons and I would have a place to live at the end of the month, even though I didn't yet know where. The best way I can describe it is as a deep inner resolve – a certainty – that just could not be shaken. I *knew* the Lord held my sons and me in the palm of His hand and that settled it for me. It was a truly uncanny peace.

Viewing our unexpected circumstances through a faith-building perspective fixes our eyes of faith on what is central – who God is. It reminds us to focus our attention on *what we do know* of God through the person of Jesus Christ, rather than on all the things we don't and can't know about our situation.

So, what can we be certain of in the midst of all our uncertainty? A revelation the apostle Paul discovered, by way of his own experience, can help us.

Like us, Paul encountered many trials and tribulations. He too met with some unexpected things in life. Just look at this list, which is by no means the full of it: "Five times I received at the hands of the Jews the forty lashes less one. Three times I was beaten with rods. Once I was stoned. Three times I was shipwrecked; a night and a day I was adrift at sea; on frequent journeys, in danger from rivers, danger from robbers, danger from my own people, danger from Gentiles, danger in the city, danger in the wilderness, danger at sea, danger from false brothers; in toil and hardship, through many a sleepless night, in hunger and thirst, often without food, in cold and exposure. And, apart from other things, there is the daily pressure on me of my anxiety for all the churches" (2 Cor 11:24–28 ESV). This man lived through some stuff!

He too was faced with the many unknowns that accompany difficult circumstances and had to navigate his way in faith through all of them. Perhaps he gives us a clue as to how he held fast to his faith in an unrelated statement he made to the Corinthians: "For I decided to know nothing among you except Jesus Christ and him crucified" (1 Cor 2:2 ESV). Here Paul reminds the Corinthians what message he preached among them, instead of relying on his human wisdom, power and eloquence[11]. But it's also a statement that reveals Paul's personal orientation towards Christ-centeredness, which is so evident throughout all his writing and ministry.

It was this unwavering pursuit of Jesus Christ – to preach Christ and Him crucified – that drove his ministry and resulted in tremendous persecution and suffering wherever he went. Perhaps the very same unwavering pursuit that led him into this adversity was also what brought him through it? His writings certainly reveal a deep personal resolve to keep Christ in view at all times:

> I have been crucified with Christ. It is no longer I who live, but Christ who lives in me. And the life I now live in the flesh, I live by faith in the Son of God, who loved me and gave himself for me (Gal 2:20 ESV).

And again:

> For to me to live is Christ, and to die is gain (Phil 1:21 ESV).

From his writings, we see evidence of Paul's perspective – he always kept his eyes of faith firmly fixed on Jesus Christ. Perhaps this is why he believed that "our light and momentary troubles are achieving for us an eternal glory that far outweighs them all" (2 Cor 4:17 NIV). How did Paul see this eternal glory that outweighs all suffering? He directs our attention to it immediately thereafter: "we fix our eyes not on what is seen, but on what is unseen, since what is seen is temporary, but what is unseen is eternal" (2 Cor 4:18 NIV). Paul had trained his eyes heavenward – to Jesus Christ – and he exhorts us to adopt the same perspective.

Paul's life and example serve as another lesson of faith. By it, we understand that if we are to move through suffering with our faith intact and in continuous cooperation with the Spirit, we must develop a resolute orientation towards Christ-centeredness. And we too must train our eyes of faith heavenward at all times and in all things – even while experiencing the unexpected things.

Stuart and I eventually got married and we did move into our new home together as a blended family. By the grace of God alone, I didn't walk away from Stuart and waited as God brought restoration to his soul. I am so grateful to the Lord for helping me to keep the lens of faith on my eyes, albeit at times rather tenuously.

Stuart is the most wonderful man of God, a great husband and an incredible father to our five children (who are now all thriving adults). The Lord did a wonderful work of healing in both of our hearts and we have just celebrated 23 years of marriage. We have both seen God's plan in bringing us together. God used our marriage to bring restoration and healing to the lives of our five children, all of whom had suffered a degree of brokenness from the breakdown of our previous marriages. If I had stopped cooperating with God, if I had let go of His hand and paused in my working together with Him, His purposes for our relationship and our family would not have been realised.

Through all of the ups and downs in our courtship, I had a keen awareness that there was a bigger picture behind all that was playing out before me. He had given me a brief glimpse of it when He showed me in a dream that I was breastfeeding two boys and a girl. That night, He invited me to partner with Him in these three children's lives and that same night, I chose to give Him my full cooperation when I gave Him my yes and responded with, "I will love them and care for them the way a mother does her own children."

God's purposes are generational (Gen 17:7; 1 Chr 16:15). They extend way beyond your lifetime here on earth. While I don't yet see in full what God will do through our marriage and blended family, the small part I do see, the part He has graciously shown me, confirms that He has tremendous purpose in our marriage for these five children's lives. I will certainly not live to see it all, but I don't have to. All He requires of me (and you for that matter) is that I continue cooperating with Him towards His end.

Chapter 10:

TRAINING OUR EYES HEAVENWARD

"So we fix our eyes not on what is seen,
but on what is unseen, since what is seen is temporary,
but what is unseen is eternal."
(2 Cor 4:18 NIV)

Training our eyes heavenward is the key to accessing a faith-building perspective. In turn, a faith-building perspective is essential to remaining in cooperation with the Holy Spirit as we navigate through the many unexpected things we will meet in this life.

Seeing past our problems and looking Christward to the unseen things requires a different perspective. If we are to engage our eyes of faith, we must learn to put away our natural lenses to see past the obvious. We must learn to see life differently.

The two-dimensional perspective represented on a road map is very different to the actual terrain we see when driving it by car. A road map zooms out and gives us a bird's-eye view of the entire area we're travelling through. But when we drive these roads by car, we see only what is within our immediate visual range – nothing beyond.

A road map serves as a great navigation tool because it allows us to see beyond our natural limitations to what lies ahead. It's a tool that helps us see the greater area and what we can't see on our own. By it, we can plot a course from one point to another without fear of making a wrong turn and losing our way. This is a real gift when it comes to planning a road trip through an unknown region, which is exactly what our fog-filled places are to us – unknown territory. In these places, a perspective greater than ours is essential because here our faith must see the unseen things (2 Cor 4:18).

The rocket ship *New Shepard* recently made history with its first successful Space Tourism flight[12]. The pricey ticket bought its passengers a unique vantage point from an altitude of 100km. Seeing the earth from this height allowed the passengers a brand new, never-seen-before view of the world. Wouldn't it be great if, like that brief visit to the boundary of space, we could glimpse our lives from heaven's window?

Unfortunately, we don't have access to an actual window in heaven, but we can construct a window of sorts. With a nod to our childhood, a simple join-the-dots illustration affords us a bird's eye-view of our life. We can imagine that, like a map, it zooms out to the bigger picture of our life. As such, it can help us see our life and the things that happen to us a little differently. It gives us that all-important new perspective.

Inserted between pages 120 and 121 is a join-the-dots activity. Depending on your personality, you might want to start connecting the dots right away to see what picture it uncovers! Please resist this temptation because the process I want you to go through is as important as discovering what lies underneath all those dots. If you patiently follow me in this exercise, you will discover some marvellous spiritual insights concerning your own life journey.

But first, a quick disclaimer: this is just a simple exercise of perspective. It's not what the bigger picture of your life looks like through the eyes of heaven. It's just a simple illustration that helps us to see our lives differently. It's also meant to be fun!

The name of this game is The Unexpected Things: it's a game of perspective.

To get started, you will need a pencil, eraser and one coloured Koki pen. You will also need to dust off your rusty childhood imagination. To get the most out of this game, do each step of the activity and then come back to read the next paragraph. Ready?

Let the game begin!

1. Consider the image on the fold out page inserted between pages 120 and 121. (This page is a tear-out for ease of reference as you work through the activity).

Beneath all these dots lies a picture. Right now, it looks like a mass of numbered dots and makes no sense whatsoever. In fact, the dots appear to be randomly scattered across the page without any real thought or design. But within that mass of strewn dots lays a very clear and strategic intention on the part of its designer – a definite picture. With the dots unconnected, we cannot yet fathom what the picture will look like.

Rules of Engagement:

- Imagine that God is the artist; He designed this picture.
- Imagine that the mass of numbered dots is a two-dimensional, bird's eye-view of your entire life – it represents your destiny in Christ. See it as the blueprint for your life and write your name at the top of the page.
- Imagine that every dot symbolises a crucial detail of your life. Each dot represents an important link in the collective chain of dots that equals the sum of your life from beginning to end.

- Imagine that this is an eternal picture that will live forever.

Your task, should you choose to accept it (cue *Mission Impossible* music in the background), is to connect all your dots to uncover the picture your life will reveal for all eternity – to His glory and for His divine purposes.

Hopefully, your imagination has been fired up by the game, so let's proceed to the next step.

2. With a pencil, circle dot 1 and dot 359.

There are 359 dots in total. Note that the dots are sequentially numbered. Imagine that every dot represents a point in your life. If dot 1 represented your birth and dot 359 your death, then all the dots in between represent the unique details and seasons that characterise your life. Each dot (season) is specifically designed and strategically placed to make up the whole of it. Because of this, each dot must be connected in sequence. This means that dot 3 must connect to dot 4, which then connects to dot 5 and so on.

To skip dots is to skip important parts of your life. Skipping dots will leave holes in the finished picture – the rhino will end up without its horn, missing an eye and balancing only on three legs!

At this point, some of us are beginning to get a bit nervous! But let's soldier on.

3. Still with a pencil, join dots 1 to 33. (Connect these dots before you read on).

With these lines drawn in, can you tell what the picture is yet?

Come on, have a guess! I know you want to. While you might want to take a stab at it, all it will be at this point is an assumption. We can apply our imagination to what it could possibly be. Perhaps a flower, a butterfly or a crab's claw? But we cannot yet identify it with any degree of certainty. To glimpse the picture that lies beneath the dots, we'll have to join many more.

Yet, this is what we often do. We tend to make assumptions about our lives based on what we know at dot 33 of our journey. Meanwhile, we still have another 326 dots to live through. If we live dot-to-dot, one season at a time, how can we hope, at dot 33, to know the whole of what will only be fully uncovered by dot 359? How can we begin to understand the full purpose of seasons 1 to 33 when we have not yet connected to dot 34 and beyond to get an idea of what God is doing with our lives?

Like my young sons, we expend a lot of energy trying to discover the undiscoverable: "Ooh, it's a flower! Umm... No, a crab! No, a rhino! Come on... It has to be a rhino!" Although this guessing game is a lot of fun for kids, when it comes to our life's picture, it's completely unnecessary. We place enormous pressure on ourselves to get our life's purpose all figured out and define our picture, when in truth we simply cannot determine the full picture from our current position, especially when we still have several other dots to join.

Write what you think the picture is at the top of the page.

4. Notice the dot sequence between dots 26–31.

At dot 27, something unexpected happened: we took an unanticipated turn in the opposite direction to dot 28. From dots 29 to 30 and 31, we drew in a zigzag.

Having only connected to dot 33, our zigzag looks out of place. Did the artist lose his way here? Perhaps he got a bit confused about the picture he was drawing. At this point of our dot journey, the zigzag appears nonsensical. We wonder at its placement within our story and might even consider it a horrible mistake.

Perhaps Joseph wondered the same thing when his life zigzagged like this? There he was, the apple of his father's eye, walking around in his expensive coat of many colours (Gen 37:3–4). From this favoured position, his life was surely heading only one way – up. After all, wasn't he spared the menial tasks his brothers did (v. 12)? Wasn't he set apart from all the others? He was special for sure and he knew it. Besides, God had even confirmed this to him in a dream, not once, but twice (vv. 5–11)!

One day, he is sent by his father to find his brothers with their sheep and suddenly his anticipated upward trajectory takes an unexpected turn. A weird dot sequence moves him in a seemingly contradictory direction. Previously, he was a celebrated son, destined for greatness and at the very next dot place, he is sold into slavery because of his brothers' betrayal (vv. 23–28).

Haven't we all had similar zigzag experiences in life? Maybe ours weren't as dramatic as Joseph's, but nonetheless they were just as confusing. We were heading in a certain direction, holding onto the dreams we received from God, and then something unexpected happened, and we found ourselves going in the wrong direction. A slave is as opposite to a ruler as you can possibly get.

From our natural perspective, a zigzag dot connection is disconcerting. Anything that unsettles us has a significant impact on our faith and cooperation with God. Often when we meet this type of dot sequence in our lives, our cooperation levels plunge, leaving our faith stranded.

We don't know what went through Joseph's mind on that long walk to the selling blocks in Egypt, but sharing his humanity, I'm pretty sure it must have been something along the lines of: "What on earth is going on, God?" or "How could you let this happen to me?"

These zigzag places in my journey have been a stumbling point in my own faith and cooperation with God. When things just don't add up or worse, seem to be unravelling and taking me way off my anticipated course – the course towards God's promises – I struggle to work together with the Spirit. Here the temptation to fix my eyes on the obvious, what is happening immediately around me, rather than on God, is greatest. Here my devastating circumstances seem to loom larger than my God. In this vulnerable place, remaining in faith and fixing my eyes on the unseen becomes a real struggle.

When things don't make sense to us, when they don't align with what we anticipate, it creates the opportunity for doubt to settle over our faith. Unconvinced that this dot sequence is useful to our picture, we're reluctant to continue our ongoing cooperation with God.

This imagined view of our life can help us with our struggle. Seeing this image laid out before us in full, we can clearly see that we have only connected dot 1 to dot 33. We can understand why we can't yet see the meaning of this zigzag within the greater design. From here, we see that there are many more dots to come and we're inclined to trust the artist's intention and imagine that it can be useful toward the end purpose.

As our game later reveals, this confusing dot sequence is deliberate. This is why, when it comes to our own lives, partnership with the Spirit is crucial. If He is leading our dot connections, then we have no reason to let go of His hand when we meet the zigzags in life. Instead, we can rest in the knowledge that the one who knows the mind of the great artist is leading the way:

> For who knows a person's thoughts except their own spirit within them? In the same way, no one knows the thoughts of God except the Spirit of God. What we have received is not the spirit of the world, but the Spirit who is from God, so that we may understand what God has freely given us (1 Cor 2:11–12 NIV).

As Joseph walked towards slavery in Egypt, bloodied and bruised (inside and out), he had no idea how God would use this turn of events in his life. From where he stood on the bidding floor, it looked hopeless; it looked like the end of all the plans God had revealed to him in his dreams.

Similarly, we don't know how all our zigzags are going to be used in the drawing of our life. From our perspective, it can look quite hopeless. Sometimes it even looks like the end of all the precious promises God has given us. Only as we journey further along, connecting more dots, will we begin to see its relevance. And here's the thing, we might only be able to tell when we get to the very last dot on the page – we just don't know when it will become clear.

Sometimes we can look back on these types of dot sequences and catch a glimpse of how God has already used them in our story. At other times, even in hindsight, we can't make head or tail of it. But as we stay in cooperation with Him, we have His faithful promise that He is working everything together for His good purposes (Rom 8:28).

God knew exactly how He would work through Joseph's unexpected circumstances. God was never limited by anything that happened to Joseph in Egypt in bringing His purposes for Joseph's life to fulfilment. If we will stay in partnership with Him the way Joseph did, we too will be able to testify that what is meant as evil against us, God will instead use for His good purposes (Gen 50:20). It's important that we don't let go of His hand during these times. We need to hold on tight and keep following Him closely. In the hand of God, all these mysterious dot sequences carry tremendous value for our overall story.

5. **Using a different colour, draw a line from dot 33 straight to dot 62, purposefully missing out all the numbers in between.**

6. **Change back to your original colour and go back to join dot 33 through to dot 62 in the proper number sequence. (Don't skip any numbers.)**

Look at the contrast between the wrong connecting line (the different colour) and the correct one. The difference is significant.

When we let go of the hand of the Spirit, we are effectively joining our own dots. We seize control of our life. From our limited perspective, we start drawing in our own lines, missing out many vital dot connections along the way. Some of us had a moment right here! It brings it home, doesn't it?

The value of perspective can only be known by those who recognise that they are limited. Dear friend, we are severely limited without the partnership of the Holy Spirit. Perhaps this is why the Lord insisted that it was to our advantage that He had to leave us and the Holy Spirit would come in His place (John 16:7). The Lord knew firsthand that we couldn't do life without the essential help of His Spirit!

Our childhood illustration has numbered dots that makes it easy for us to follow the sequence. But our life doesn't work this way. From our viewpoint, we don't see all our days laid out before us and there are no numbers guiding us through the seasons of life. We have no idea which dot we are currently at and which dot comes next – only God knows this. When we blunder along alone, without the indispensable help of the Spirit, we effectively draw in our own lines. And when we draw a straight line from dot 33 to 62, skipping out all the necessary dots in between, a work of recovery is required.

According to the Oxford dictionary, recovery means to regain possession of something stolen or lost[13]. When something has been lost or stolen from our overall picture, it must be recovered, so that when our final picture is revealed, our rhino is sporting its horn and standing on all four of its legs.

Directing our own paths by what we can see and understand is dangerous. What we perceive to be the right path might turn out to be the wrong direction, at times with devastating effect. This is what Adam and Eve did when they disobeyed God and ate from the forbidden tree. With limited vision, they drew in their own line, effectively plunging all of humankind into sin (Gen 3). The wonderful message of the gospel is God's subsequent response of recovery. He sent His only Son, Jesus Christ, to recover all that had been lost to humanity through this disastrous dot connection (John 3:16; Rom 3:23–24). This is a great place to pause and praise God for the redeeming work of His Son and to appreciate His ongoing work of recovery in our daily lives (Ps 23:1–3).

Whenever we go about connecting our own dots, we have to pause in our progression to allow Him to restore what has been lost. The long gap between the Fall and the cross is testament to this principle.

Making our own way comes at a hefty price. We incur loss. Some believers spend more time recovering what has been lost because of their disobedience (Prov 1:15; Jer 7:23; 18:15) than progressing along the right path for their lives (John 17:4). But if we stay in cooperation with Him and pursue His ways, He can help us complete our unique picture that will stand for eternity (1 Kings 6:12; Heb 10:36).

So, are you ready to resist joining your own dots? Are you willing to surrender and press into ongoing cooperation with Him who knows all the details of your life? I pray the Lord helps us to.

7. Place a small circle around dot 22 and dot 125.

Imagine that, like Joseph, God gives you a glimpse into your future at dot 22. Let's say that at dot 22, you too have a dream of sorts. It might be a word from God or prophecy that gives direction to your life. But it is profound, as was the case with Joseph, who had two distinctly similar dreams (Gen 37:6–9) and you know without a doubt that God is speaking to you about your life.

Imagine that dot 125 represents the point in your journey where that dream is destined to come to pass. That dot represents fulfilment, the time when you will come into what you only caught a glimpse of at dot 22.

Between dot 22 and dot 125 are 103 other dots. These dots represent the waiting period between receiving the dream and the fulfilment of it. They are the necessary seasons that must pass between "foretaste" dot 22 and "fulfilment" dot 125.

From our natural viewpoint, we cannot see our "fulfilment" dot places. We can only see the now and what has already passed through our many yesterdays. All we have is the dream – whatever its form. We have no way of knowing exactly when it will come to pass in our lives. We don't have a birds-eye-view of our lives, with the "fulfilment" dot neatly identified in a circle.

Often, after God gives us a glimpse of our future, we anticipate that it will come to pass soon – if not in our current position, then surely just one or two dots later? We assume that if He chose to show it to us now, it must be for now. But, as Joseph discovered, there are many dots and zigzags to journey through before we come to the fulfilment of that promise.

Lying between the dreams God gave Joseph as a boy to the time of their fulfilment were a multitude of unexpected seasons. It's reasonable to assume that at times Joseph must have questioned if that dream was from God at all. As a slave in Egypt, his circumstances were so far from the promise of that dream that he might have been tempted to abandon it entirely. Instead of others bowing down to him, he was the slave having to bow to others (Gen 39:1).

But this was not the end of Joseph's dream; there were many more dots to live through before he could come to the place of fulfilment (Gen 41:41; 42:6). At the point of his betrayal and being sold into slavery, however, all Joseph could see were the shattered shards of his God-given dreams.

This illustration helps us to understand that what we experience at any given point in our lives is only a small part of the much larger whole. By it, we learn the futility of leaning on our own understanding and are again pointed towards the importance of partnering with the Holy Spirit (Prov 3:5-6).

8. With your pencil, jump ahead to dot 125 where your dream is fulfilled and join from there to 170. Leave out all the dots from 62 to 124.

Does the newly connected section make any further sense of the overall picture? Does jumping ahead to dot 125, where the fulfilment of your God-given dream takes place, and connecting it to later numbers enable you to see what the picture is?

No, it doesn't. Why? As much as we look forward to this future point in our lives, it doesn't reveal the underlying picture because it remains disconnected from the rest of our journey.

In light of this, consider the value of every individual dot. The artist has placed each dot in its place for a reason – each one is necessary to uncover the whole. It's the artist's intention that every dot carries purpose.

Purpose is defined by the Merriam-Webster dictionary as "something set up as an object or end to be attained"[14]. Uncovering the picture that lies beneath our dots is an end to be attained, but it isn't the only one. Connecting every specific dot in the correct sequence is also an end that must be attained. As part of this game, there are a number of goals – 359 of them, to be exact.

One of the reasons we run ahead, skipping dots and drawing in our own lines is that we fail to appreciate that each dot place in our story holds tremendous value. Dot 300 is no more important than dot 2, while dot 15 is no less significant than dot 115. There are no dots on this page that are more or less important than any other. They hold equal value in the pattern that lies before us as we attempt to uncover it in full.

The purpose of our life can't only become significant at dot 322 or at any other anticipated point in our future. Rather, every dot in our story is a place of purpose. Not one dot, on our personal page of destiny in Christ, is irrelevant to our purpose. All 359 dots are needed to make up the whole picture.

Let's follow this thought a little further. If I'm a disciple of Jesus Christ and am following Him daily (Matt 16:24), then I can never be in a dot place (season) in my life that is detached from my purpose and destiny in Him.

If I've made a decision to give my life to Christ...

> That which is born of the flesh is flesh, and that which is born of the Spirit is spirit. Do not marvel that I said to you, 'You must be born again' (John 3:6-8 ESV).

> Jesus replied, 'I am the way, and the truth, and the life. No one comes to the Father except through me' (John 14:6 ESV).

And if I'm still following Him...

> But seek first the kingdom of God and his righteousness, and all these things will be added to you (Matt 6:33 ESV).

Then I'm fulfilling my purpose in Him.

> Now all has been heard; here is the conclusion of the matter: Fear God and keep his commandments, for this is the duty of all mankind (Eccl 12:13 NIV).

> So whether you eat or drink or whatever you do, do it all for the glory of God (1 Cor 10:31 NIV).

This means that every dot on my page is filled with opportunities to fulfil God's purpose for my life. It replaces the idea that our life's purpose officially starts at a specific point. Instead of chasing that elusive dot where everything will suddenly fall in place, we understand that we're already living it daily.

When we see each dot as a significant part of our whole story, the present becomes increasingly important. We start appreciating our todays more; we learn to place high value on them. No longer will we only count the big events of our life as significant. We will see significance in all of it, even the small and mundane, and yes, even the unexpected things.

This emphasises the importance of our daily cooperation with the Holy Spirit. If today is full of purpose, then I'm mindful not to treat it carelessly. Instead of wishing my current position away in search of the next significant season, I slow down and press in closer to my partner. I seek ever-increasing cooperation with the only one who knows the pattern and sequence of all my dots (1 Cor 2:10–11). Grateful for His divine help, we hold on tighter and push in closer as we follow His lead (Rom 8:14).

This reveals the tremendous value of our daily lives. Each day is filled with the opportunity to fulfil God's purposes for us. Recognising that every place in our journey has a purpose is a powerful revelation. Embracing it will set us free from the need to define ourselves by one specific place in our journey or by certain events. Instead, we allow God to use our daily lives to accomplish His magnificent purposes.

How many dots do you think you've already connected? Depending on your age, you might be able to estimate how far along you think you are in your dot journey. The longer you have lived, the further along you may be. Are you halfway, a little less or a little more?

Revisit the name of the picture you previously wrote at the top of the page. Do you still think it represents that? If not, write another title just under it.

9. Place a triangle around the dot you think you are at right now.

Imagine that each dot represents a time span or a season. Before us, we see 359 dots, which means that our life represented here consists of 359 seasons or time spans. God controls the timing of these seasons: some are short, some are long, but only He knows the length of each (Job 14:5; Acts 17:26).

Right now, we have no idea how long we'll be at the point we just enclosed with a triangle. Moses' first wilderness dot lasted for 40 years before he was commissioned to leave Midian and go to Egypt (his next dot) where he confronted Pharoah (Acts 7:30). Then, after leading the Israelites out of Egypt, he spent another 40 years wandering around the wilderness again because of their unbelief (Num 14:28–25; Acts 13:18).

Each dot holds equal value, but not equal time. The plans of God unfold in real time, not ahead of time. Moses didn't get prior notice from God, notifying him that after tending his flock for 40 years in the desert, he would then return to Egypt to free His people. This was all unfolding for Moses in real time, as he journeyed through his daily life following God.

We don't know how long we'll be in our current position for. We also don't know how many dots make up our story. Each of us have a page with a different number of dots on it. Before us, we see a series of 359 dots, but our life story may contain hundreds more, depending on how long we live.

10. Consider the view from your current dot.

Let's zoom in for a moment to consider the perspective from our current dot. Take a look at the image below.

Image 1.1

Imagine that this is our view from our current dot. We are travelling on a dirt road and have no idea where it will lead us to. We can see the road stretching ahead of us and the green bushes on either side. More than this, we can't see. This is the limit of our understanding of where we are. We don't even know what lies over the next hill. We will only see more when we travel further on.

Now compare this view to the photo below.

Image 1.2

Here we have an aerial view of the area in which we're travelling. We have a bird's-eye view of the full extent of a city: its roads, waterways, parks, houses and skyscrapers all clearly laid out before us. Imagine that the stretch of dirt road, which is our current dot (Image 1.1), is a road that will eventually lead us to this city. However, from our current dot, we can't see any of this. We're unaware that we're travelling towards a city – all we see is a stretch of road before us. From our current position, today is still unfolding and we don't know what our tomorrow holds (Jas 4:12–14).

Much like this aerial view, God sees our current dot within the framework of the bigger picture for our lives. He sees everything that surrounds us and lies beyond us; it's all laid out before Him from beginning to end (Ps 139:16; Rev 1:8).

In comparing these two perspectives, the difference in terms of what can be seen is significant. God knows that He is leading us to a city – we do not. God knows the safest route to the city – we do not. God sees it all before Him – we see only a stretch of road ahead. It makes little sense then to rely on our limited ability to connect to our next dot.

The comparison highlights the importance of our cooperation with the Holy Spirit, who is the only one on earth who sees the bigger picture of our lives (1 Cor 2:10). He sees all that lies beyond the current road we're travelling. If we cooperate closely with Him, we can have absolute confidence that He'll show us the best way forward.

11. Place a square around dot number 84.

Let us zoom in again to a specific place, dot 84, where we meet something unexpected. In this season, something we didn't see coming happens and we find ourselves in a hard place.

Consider the following image:

Image 1.3

Imagine that this is what the unexpected looks like. We suddenly encounter this enormous rockface that obscures our view and hinders our way. No matter which way we look, all we see is solid rock and the steep mountain we must climb.

This immovable wall of rock could represent a myriad different things – if it was unexpected and left you reeling, then it falls into the category of the unexpected things.

Now compare this view to the one opposite:

Image 1.4

Here we have an aerial view that allows us to see beyond the sheer mountain face. We're able to glimpse what lies beyond it – the full mountain range with all its valleys. We notice that what first appeared as a dead end (Image 1.3) is in fact a small part of a much greater picture. The mountain that once loomed large in our lives is now small and seemingly insignificant. Why? Because of the change in perspective.

When comparing the two images, the benefit that the aerial view affords is undeniable. From this vantage point, the solid wall of rock (Image 1.3) is contextualised within the Creator's larger design. Without this bigger perspective, we might well resign ourselves to the hopelessness of the insurmountable wall, imagining that there's no way around it. Restricted to our limited perspective (Image 1.3), we easily succumb to the faith-eroding conclusion that there is no way to overcome it.

What if, at the time we came face to face with that solid wall we could also see it situated within God's larger design for our lives? What if, in our utter despair, we could glimpse all that lies beyond the rockface and see a clear way over it? How would this alter our perception of that formidable wall of rock?

I believe it might give us hope that all is not lost. It might strengthen us to believe that the God who sees everything (Gen 16:13) can certainly bring us over this immovable wall. He can certainly work this unexpected thing into His plans and purposes for our lives (Rom 8:28). It might allow us to imagine that what appears to us as an insurmountable mountain could to God be little more than a plain (Zech 4:7). How might this new perspective change things for you?

When it comes to our faith, contextualising the immediacy of the unexpected things (sheer rockface) within the bigger picture of God's sovereignty over our lives (the full mountain range) is indispensable. Through the eyes of faith, we see our unexpected things differently. We see the seemingly insurmountable wall of rock juxtaposed against the awesomeness of our God. Now our faith has something larger than itself to hold fast to.

On the other hand, if the wall before us appears larger than the size of our God, then our faith is defeated and our hope of overcoming adversity is lost. We serve a big God. He is the Creator of the heavens, the earth and everything in them (Gen 1:1). What is impossible for man is possible with Him (Luke 18:27). He is the good Shepherd (John 10:11) and He won't lead us over a cliff. He died in our place (Rom 3:25) and longs to lead us beside still waters and into paths of righteousness (Ps 23). He alone knows the way we should go (Isa 30:20–21). This is very good news when we meet the unexpected things!

12. The Step You Have Been Patiently Waiting For

Go ahead and join all the dots to the end to see what the picture will uncover. But before you rush to do that, remember to invite the Holy Spirit into your exercise, so that He can give you even further insight into your own dot journey with Him.

13. The End of Our Game

Did you guess correctly as to what the final picture would be? A few of you might have, but for most of us, it only became apparent around halfway through the exercise.

Perspective is a powerful tool. It frames our world and determines our perceptions. In this way, a different perspective brings new understanding. By it, we understand that we don't see and know it all. We see and know only a tiny fragment of the vast whole of God and His ways (1 Cor 13:12; Isa 55:8–9). A new perspective strengthens our faith and reminds us to train our eyes heavenward when our circumstances don't make any sense. We fix our eyes on a sovereign God who set the moon and stars in place (Ps 8:3). Thanks to perspective, we recognise the foolishness of our best human efforts to fathom the unfathomable:

> But how can mere mortals prove their innocence before God?
> Though they wished to dispute with him,
> they could not answer him one time out of a thousand.
> His wisdom is profound, his power is vast.
> Who has resisted him and come out unscathed?
> He moves mountains without their knowing it
> and overturns them in his anger.

> He shakes the earth from its place
> and makes its pillars tremble.
> He speaks to the sun and it does not shine;
> he seals off the light of the stars.
> He alone stretches out the heavens
> and treads on the waves of the sea.
> He is the Maker of the Bear and Orion,
> the Pleiades and the constellations of the south.
> He performs wonders that cannot be fathomed,
> miracles that cannot be counted.
> When he passes me, I cannot see him;
> when he goes by, I cannot perceive him.
> If he snatches away, who can stop him?
> Who can say to him, "What are you doing?" (Job 9:2–12 NIV)

So far, our game of perspective has challenged the way we view our life in Christ. I hope this game has led you to a "burning bush"' encounter with God (Exod 3). Perhaps God is using a children's join-the-dots illustration to grab our attention in the hope that we, like Moses, will turn to hear what He is saying (v. 3).

The burning bush signalled a turning point in Moses' life (Exod 3). If we look past the miracle of the burning bush, we find out why. Although a bush on fire that doesn't burn would be a wonderful miracle, if we look past the obvious, we find that the purpose of the burning-bush moment was ultimately an *invitation*.

God wanted to show His love for His beloved people (Exod 3:7). He wanted to set them free from their brutal captivity in Egypt (v. 8). But He needed a partner who would work with Him to accomplish His plan. He chose Moses and invites him to cooperate with Him (v. 10). Reluctantly at first, Moses finally accepts and then works together with God to achieve His end.

Similarly, if we look past the fun of our join-the-dots game, we find that God's purpose in it is also an invitation. An invitation for our partnership. An invitation to cooperate with His plans for our lives on the earth. You see, if by this game, we come to an understanding of just how helpless we are in directing our own lives, then it can, like Moses' burning bush, mark a critical point in our life too. We can accept His invitation and give Him our ongoing cooperation towards His ends. We can place our trust in Him, in His goodness and love, even when the unexpected things happen.

This exercise has allowed us to juxtapose God's perspective alongside ours. His ways are so very different to our own (Isa 55:8–9). We are largely focused on today and what is happening around us. However, God's focus is eternal (Rev 22:5). We want to achieve our goals immediately or in the near future. God is never in a rush (2 Pet 3:8). We have limits. He is unlimited (Matt 19:26).

It's my prayer that this join-the-dots image will forever remain etched in our minds. Whether we find ourselves on the dirt road or at the mountain face, we can choose to embrace a bigger perspective that will help us to partner better with the Holy Spirit.

Chapter 11:

PERSONAL REFLECTION

"There's far more here than meets the eye.
The things we see now are here today, gone tomorrow.
But the things we can't see now will last forever."
(2 Cor 4:18 MSG)

God has not called believers to a life of sight – He has called us to a life of faith (2 Cor 5:7). And faith resides in the unseen things (Heb 11:1). If we are to live a life of faith, we must invite the Holy Spirit to lift our spiritual eyes heavenward, so that we can find the right lens to examine our current situation.

The handle of perspective grounds our faith in the principle of the bigger picture. When we hold fast to it, we place our faith on the unshakable ground that our God is much greater than whatever crisis we may face.

If we are to have any hope of remaining in cooperation with the Holy Spirit through the fog of the unexpected things, then we must, as a matter of habit, cultivate a faith-building perspective.

A prepared faith is a protected faith. We must familiarise ourselves with a faith-building perspective today, so that when we meet a crisis tomorrow, our faith is not left scrambling to find the right lens. A protected faith is not left vulnerable to the enemy's many faith-eroding strategies.

Putting It Into Practice: Handle of Perspective

Spiritual Insight: My ongoing cooperation with the Holy Spirit requires a faith-building perspective.

1. Read Job 11:7–9 and 1 Corinthians 13:12. How does this change the way you view circumstances in your life that don't make sense?

2. Like Job's friends, we've all been caught in the trap of trying to label and explain things that lie beyond our human understanding. Recall one instance when you got caught up in trying to explain the unexplainable things. What were the consequences?

3. Read Hebrews 11:1–31. What is the common pattern of perspective among these great men and women of faith?

4a). Read Matthew 7:15–20, John 10:10 and James 1:17. How does this help you keep a true image of God when you meet adversity?

b) Looking back at the unexpected things in your life, when did you blame God for things that happened to you? If so, take a moment to repent. Then ponder the ways you can keep His goodness constantly before you as you reset.

5. When we view our unexpected circumstances through the right lens, it builds our faith. List three ways our faith finds strength when we look through the lens of God.

6a) What was your biggest "aha" moment as you worked through the join-the-dots activity?

b) In response to this, what are some of the changes the Lord is inviting you to make?

7) Consider the dot you find yourself at right now. Are you in an unexpected place? Spend some time reading through the lyrics of this timeless hymn, written by Helen Howarth Lemmel. Meditate on the chorus in particular. You might even want to sing it aloud.

O soul, are you weary and troubled?
No light in the darkness you see
There's light for a look at the Saviour
And life more abundant and free

Turn your eyes upon Jesus
Look full in His wonderful face
And the things of earth will grow strangely dim
In the light of His glory and grace

His word shall not fail you, He promised
Believe Him and all will be well
Then go to a world that is dying
His perfect salvation to tell

Turn your eyes upon Jesus
Look full in His wonderful face
And the things of earth will grow strangely dim
In the light of His glory and grace

O soul, are you weary and troubled?
No light in the darkness you see
There's light for a look at the Saviour
And life more abundant and free

Turn your eyes upon Jesus
Look full in His wonderful face
And the things of earth will grow strangely dim
In the light of His glory and grace.
(*Turn Your Eyes Upon Jesus* by Helen Howarth Lemmel)

8. a) After meditating on these lyrics, does your unexpected thing look the same to you?

b) Describe how it is now different.
c) Why do you think this is?

SECTION 3:
HANDLE OF PERSEVERANCE

"But if we hope for what we do not see, we wait for it with patience."
(Rom 8:25 ESV)

Our join-the-dots illustration has allowed us to imagine God's bigger picture for our lives. Hopefully, this exercise of perspective has begun to help us view our life and the things that happen to us along the way a little differently. This is an important exercise if we are to cultivate a faith-building perspective.

However, if we are to be counted among the overcomers (Rev 21:7), among those who keep going and overcome through the unexpected things, we will also need the handle of perseverance.

Let's recap on how we've already begun planning for the unplanned. In equipping our faith with the tools its needs to meet the unexpected things, we've identified that our partnership with the Holy Spirit is indispensable. We must cooperate with the only one who can lead us through the unknown (1 Cor 2:11).

We've noted the impact our perspective has on our faith (Heb 11:1). Our understanding of our situation is either strengthening our faith in God or eroding it. Cultivating a faith-building perspective is critical; it tethers us to the unshakable truth that our God is much greater than whatever crisis we face.

Both of these spiritual disciplines are necessary, but without our third handle – perseverance – neither are very effective in bringing us through the unexpected things.

Faith, without perseverance, can't go very far. Recall my terrifying experience of having to drive home in the dense fog as a teenager. Using this illustration, let's say the car I was driving in represents the Holy Spirit. He is the vehicle – the strength that carries us through our journey of faith in Christ (2 Cor 4:7). If the car represents the Holy Spirit, then driving the car stands for our partnership with Him.

Following this line of thinking, the headlights represent a faith-building perspective. By turning them on, we're able to shine a light on what lies ahead. The petrol is our faith. It fuels the forward momentum of the car, our faith working and moving us ahead in our journey with Christ.

Our third handle, perseverance, is like the necessary action of keeping our foot firmly on the accelerator, so that fuel is continually fed into the engine. If I lift my foot off the accelerator, the car can't move forward. I've stopped. And if we're stationary, we can't move through the fog of our circumstances – no matter how impressive the car may be.

When we meet the unexpected things, perseverance is the fuel that keeps us moving forward in faith with God and His purposes for our life. Faith on its own is not enough to take us all the way to the end, for it is by faith *and patience* that we inherit the promises of God (Heb 6:11). Our faith needs to learn to be patient. We need patient faith if we are to realise God's promises (Heb 6:15). And this patient waiting is in effect the effort of perseverance.

For many of us this is not particularly good news for two reasons. First, we do not like to wait. My name is first on that list! We definitely don't roll out of bed every morning looking for opportunities to exercise patiently waiting for things. Second, we tend to inwardly flinch at the mention of the word perseverance because of its unpleasant associations. A closer look at the meaning of the word might suggest why.

Perseverance is defined by the Oxford dictionary as "persistence in doing something despite difficulty or delay in achieving success"[15]. Those two words, difficulty and delay, are the offending culprits. They explain our tendency to recoil at the mention of perseverance.

We generally avoid doing something difficult, particularly when the path of least resistance is that much easier. Moreover, our modern world worships at the altar of success, so we tend to view any type of delay in attaining success as an obstacle – even an enemy – that must quickly be removed at all costs.

Perhaps a more ironic reason is that we simply don't have the time. There is just too much to get done. Who has the time to hang around persevering? I've got goals – places to go and people to see – and persevering through difficulties is simply not on the agenda! We might laugh, but sadly, this mindset leads many believers to drop out of their race for Jesus. Many take their foot off the accelerator and come to a complete standstill in their walk with Christ because they didn't fully grasp that faith means persisting *through* difficulties as we patiently wait for the Lord's deliverance.

Our join-the-dots illustration is not only an exercise in perspective, but also an exercise in perseverance. The full picture couldn't be revealed until we had patiently connected all the way to the very last dot. Working through the various stages of the game in the previous chapter was an exercise in perseverance. We had to wait until we could finally connect all the dots and achieve the success of completing it. For some, this delay was agonising. Maybe you couldn't wait and jumped ahead to connect them all! There's no shame in that, but the point is we don't like delays in achieving success.

When it comes to our journey of faith in Christ, perseverance is critical. Staying in daily cooperation with the Spirit during our lifetime, however long that will be, requires perseverance. To work with Him to achieve His ends requires daily persistence. To realise our full destiny in Christ, in partnership with His Spirit, requires perseverance. In this regard, faith and perseverance are as inseparable as faith and perspective. While the latter helps us keep our eyes fixed on God and His covenant promises, the former ensures that we realise their fulfilment:

> For in this hope, we were saved. But hope that is seen is no hope at all. Who hopes for what they already have? But if we hope for what we do not yet have, we wait for it patiently (Rom 8:24–25 NIV).

Waiting patiently in faith for what we don't yet have requires perseverance. And if we are to hold on in faith through the unexpected things until we overcome, we will need to do much of it.

Navigating the zigzags as we trust in the artist's overall design for our lives requires perseverance. We must wait patiently through them to see how God will use them for His good purpose within the greater design for our lives (Rom 8:28). Reaching our fulfilment dots calls for perseverance. We must wait patiently for the dream to come to pass in our lives. Allowing God's plans to unfold in His timing requires perseverance. Without it, we risk running ahead and connecting our own dots.

Remaining faithful through our current season requires perseverance. We can't reach our ultimate destination if we don't keep walking along the narrow stretch of road we're on right now – no matter how laborious it may seem.

Yes, perseverance is an indispensable handrail for our faith, particularly when we meet with the unexpected things. Without it, we can't progress through the dense fog and into the clearing. And progress we must, for as long as we are alive, there remains yet another dot on our journey to connect to.

The need for perseverance in our walk with God is an easy sell. Perseverance is essential, not only in the general rhythm of life, but also when it comes to our faith. Waiting in faith, for the things we don't yet see, demands our perseverance (Heb 11:1).

What is not such an easy sell is the doing of it. Practising perseverance is a much more expensive purchase. It's more difficult to apply it than to acknowledge our need for it.

Perhaps this is because perseverance requires a response and effort on our part, which don't come easily to us. It means regularly making choices that will challenge us in a number of ways. Let's take a look at some of these demands of perseverance.

Chapter 12:

CHOOSE TO TRUST

"In repentance and rest is your salvation,
in quietness and trust is your strength..."
(Isa 30:15 NIV)

The unexpected things exert enormous pressure on our lives. They force us to cope with difficult circumstances. The intensity of it all places us under extreme stress, which wear us down on all fronts: physically, emotionally and spiritually.

In the midst of crisis, we look for relief. We want the pain and suffering to end as quickly as possible. We want to come through the disorientating fog and into a clearing – a place where the pressure eases and we can finally breathe again. We desperately search for ways to get through these difficulties.

The distance between our crisis and the place of breakthrough must be covered by perseverance. If we don't keep moving forward with God, we can never arrive at our breakthrough. The way we move forward, though, is key, particularly if we want to walk in faith, which ultimately is the way of perseverance (Heb 6:12).

In the midst of the unexpected things, we have a number of options. We can choose many different ways to seek help. We can choose to follow various paths that offer help and relief. But there is a specific path that we need to travel if we are to secure the victory Christ has in store for us. And we find our way to this path by making a decision.

It's a decision that Judah failed to make when faced with adversity (Isa 28–35) and is a story that affords us valuable insight. It took place at a time when the Asian super-power, Assyria, was on the rise and had set their sights on conquering Judah, the southern kingdom of Israel.[16]

Judah was facing imminent war and devastation. Their future looked bleak. Their livelihoods were under serious threat and they had to take action. The Assyrians were too strong for them and it was clear that they needed help. But instead of turning to God and trusting Him, they turned to Egypt for help. In response, God sends His messenger Isaiah to Judah with a sobering warning:

> Ah, stubborn children," declares the LORD,
> "who carry out a plan, but not mine,
> and who make an alliance, but not of my Spirit,
> that they may add sin to sin;
> who set out to go down to Egypt,
> without asking for my direction,
> to take refuge in the protection of Pharaoh
> and to seek shelter in the shadow of Egypt! (Isa 30:1–3 ESV)

In this message, God tells Judah the following:

- You are carrying out a plan, but it is not Mine.
- You are making alliances and seeking support, but not with Me.
- You are heading in a direction without asking Me if it is the right one.
- You are looking to someone other than me for protection, provision and deliverance.

The seriousness of His rebuke finds its context within God's covenant relationship with His people. Israel and Judah were God's chosen people (Ex 19:5–6). God's covenant with Israel established Him as their protector, provider and deliverer (Deut 28:1–14). Judah's decision to turn to Egypt for protection was, in effect, a decision to turn away from their covenant relationship with God. God describes His covenant with Israel as a marriage (Jer 31:32). In choosing Egypt, Judah was essentially behaving like an unfaithful spouse towards God (Jer 3:6–10).

In situations like the one Judah was facing, God's covenant promise was clear:

> The Lord will cause your enemies who rise against you to be defeated before you. They shall come out against you one way and flee before you seven ways (Deut 28:7 ESV).

Faithful to His promises, God had delivered the Jewish people many times over. Israel had a long list of God-given conquests over her enemies, a clear track record of His covenant faithfulness (Exod 17:8–13; Num 21:3, 24, 34; Deut 2:33; Josh 6; 8:1).

Yet despite this rich history of God's faithfulness, Judah does not turn to Him in quiet trust, but instead abandons Him (Isa 30:15-17). Worse, they choose the help of mere men (Egypt) over the help of Almighty God: "The Egyptians are man, and not God, and their horses are flesh, and not spirit..." (Isa 31:3 ESV).

As a result, Judah finally succumbs to Assyria:

> In the fourteenth year of King Hezekiah's reign, Sennacherib king of Assyria attacked all the fortified cities of Judah and captured them (Isa 36:1 NIV).

In the face of adversity, Judah made a disastrous choice to rely on the strength of Egypt instead of God. In our context, Egypt represents anything that we turn to that replaces our reliance on God. Egypt is something more tangible and immediate that we can turn to, rather than taking up the posture of patient faith before God.

Egypt is something *we* can make happen. Egypt is help that is available to us right now – there is no need to persist in our difficulties or wait. Turning to Egypt means we don't need to wait for a breakthrough or persevere through hardship. And when the pressures of our circumstances crush us from all sides, the temptation to find an Egypt-type solution is high – just as it was for Judah.

Judah needed help: they had to respond to the threat of war. Similarly, when we meet the unexpected things, we too must respond – our circumstances demand it of us. We must choose what we will look to for help and strength. We must choose who and what we will place our trust in.

In our crisis places, there are many opportunities to place our trust in things other than God and His covenant promises. There are many alternatives that lead us to relying on an Egypt of some kind, instead of drawing strength from quiet trust in our faithful, covenant-keeping God (Isa 30:15).

The lesson Judah's story affords us is this: the way of perseverance begins with a decision to trust God at a time when we are sorely tempted to do whatever might appear to bring faster relief. It is the first step our faith must take if we are to travel the path of patient perseverance and inherit the promises of God (Heb 6:12). This will lead us to our breakthrough:

> Trust in the Lord with all your heart and lean not on your own understanding; in all your ways submit to him, and he will make your paths straight (Prov 3:5-6 NIV).

By placing their trust in Egypt instead of God, Judah leant on their own understanding and, as a result, were defeated. Consider how this story might have turned out differently if Judah had turned in faith to God instead of relying on Egypt. Could He have come to their rescue as He'd done before on so many occasions? Could they have defeated Assyria the same way Joshua defeated Amalek by the strength of the Lord (Exod 17:8–13)? Could they have overpowered the King of Assyria the way they did the Canaanites (Num 21:3), Amorites (v. 24) and Og the king of Bashan (v. 34)? Perhaps God would have given Assyria over to Judah the way He gave the city of Jericho to Joshua (Josh 6) or with a similar ambush strategy, the way Israel took Ai (Josh 8:1–29). The list of possibilities of how God could have given them victory over Assyria goes on and on as we recall Israel's history of supernatural victories over their enemies – had they only turned to Him.

But Judah didn't turn to God. They turned to Egypt. And Egypt couldn't give them the victory they so desperately needed.

Today, as we seek to respond to our crushing circumstances, let's make sure that we don't make the same mistake that Judah did. The breakthrough we so desperately seek is only realised through persistently trusting in God. We must keep moving forward in faith with God if we are to ever come out of the fog of our difficulty and into the clearing of His divine promises of deliverance.

Perseverance begins with a decision to trust God. It's a decision accompanied with God's promise to make our path straight (Prov 3:6). God yearns to direct us through our painful difficulties. The Holy Spirit longs to take us by the hand and lead us onto the straight path. This is the path of faith in Christ, it's the only path that leads to life (John 6:51) and we walk it by way of perseverance (Luke 21:19).

Perseverance is not a once-off resolution. A decision to persevere today doesn't guarantee that tomorrow we'll still be waiting in quiet trust (Isa 30:15). Unfortunately, we aren't that consistent. Only God is unchanging (Heb 13:8). One moment we're up and the next we're down. One day we're standing firm in faith and boldly declaring God's promises and the next day we're drowning in a sea of doubt and unbelief (2 Tim 2:13).

To keep ourselves in quiet trust, we must habitually make a number of other decisions.

Chapter 13:

CHOOSE THE MORE DIFFICULT OPTION

"Enter through the narrow gate."

(MATT 7:13A NIV)

Although it may seem like the more attractive option, easy is not always best. Yet despite this, we don't like the difficult option and are less likely to pursue it. Often we run in the opposite direction of difficult options. We would much rather exhaust all the easy options first. Choosing the more difficult option is often our last resort when none of the other options have worked out.

Choosing the way of trust and faith in Christ is always the more difficult option for our flesh. It's more difficult because it's the intangible option, the timing and context of which we have absolutely no control over.

Our faith in God has us walking a road much like this one:

We don't know where or when this road ends. We don't know what lies just around the bend that we can see ahead.

Despite these unknowns, trusting God means we must choose to stay on this road. Our faith must keep putting one foot in front of the other for as long as He has us walking on it – even when it becomes tiresome and we feel it's taking too long to come into God's promises. This is the more difficult way of perseverance.

We chose to walk this way when we received Jesus Christ as our Lord and Saviour:

> Enter by the narrow gate. For the gate is wide and the way is easy that leads to destruction, and those who enter by it are many. For the gate is narrow and *the way is hard that leads to life*, and those who find it are few (Matt 7:13-14 ESV).

We entered through the narrow gate when we accepted Jesus Christ as the only way to God and eternal life (John 14:6–7). We are walking on the narrow road of faith in Christ and we must keep making many more difficult choices as we put off our former ways to conform to His (Luke 9:23; Rom 6:3; Gal 2:20; 5:24; Eph 4:22).

Our faith continually demands difficult choices from us. We must believe in a God that we can't see and stand on promises that are as yet unfulfilled (Heb 11:1). It's far easier to concede that if we can't see it, we won't believe it, but we aren't called to this broad road. We're called to the less travelled, more difficult road of faith (Rom 8:13).

The broad road – the easier, less tiring and more convenient road – lies in the opposite direction to the hard way of persevering in faith. Often it's our pursuit of this convenience that pulls us off the path of perseverance. We grow tired of putting one foot in front of the other on this hard road, day in and day out. We grow tired of waiting patiently for God. We grow tired of trusting Him to fulfil His promises.

The broad, convenient road is the one Christ calls us to forsake as His disciples (Matt 10:38). Instead, He invites us to keep choosing the more difficult way – to enter into His promises through the narrow gate and to keep walking along this demanding road by faith.

Abraham chose the more difficult option when he left his own country that was comfortable and familiar to journey with God to an unknown land (Gen 12:1; Acts 7:2–3; Heb 11:8). Similarly, the widow Ruth made a difficult choice when she left Moab and followed her mother-in-law Naomi back to Bethlehem (Ruth 1:16).

In exile, Daniel had to make a number of difficult choices in order to remain faithful to God and not submit to the ways of the Babylonians. Putting himself at risk, he chose not to eat the king's delicacies (Dan 1:8) and to continue praying, even when it meant he would be thrown in a den of lions (6:10; 16). What about the difficult choice his friends Hananiah, Mishael and Azariah made when they refused to bow down and worship the golden statue Nebuchadnezzar had erected (Dan 3:18)? This decision of faith resulted in their being thrown into a fiery furnace (v. 21).

And let's not forget the prophet Jeremiah, who chose to prophesy the unpopular truth that Jerusalem would be conquered by Babylon (Jer 21:7). Because of that decision, he faced fierce opposition, death and imprisonment (26:11; 37:15; 38:4–6). Or think about Mary when she said yes to God's invitation to give birth to Jesus, knowing that as an unmarried woman, she would sacrifice her reputation (Luke 1:30–37).

Each of these biblical characters grappled with difficult decisions. These hard choices kept them on the narrow, less travelled road of faith (Matt 7:13–14). Step by step, they needed to persevere as they placed their trust in God alone. In the same way, we are called by Christ to follow the same difficult road of faith (Luke 9:23–24).

Chapter 14:

CHOOSE TO WAIT LONGER THAN WE WANT TO

"But if we hope for something we do not yet see,
we must learn how to wait for it."
(Rom 8:25 NLV)

God's calendar is not the same as ours. He doesn't perceive time the same way we do:

> But do not overlook this one fact, beloved, that with the Lord one day is as a thousand years, and a thousand years as one day (2 Pet 3:8 ESV).

In this verse, Peter addresses the false accusation that God doesn't deliver on His promises. He warns us that there will be those who mock our faith as they point out all the unfulfilled promises of God, such as the Lord's return to earth (v. 4).

In his reply, Peter emphasises the bigger picture (Is 55:8) as he points us to God's higher ways. God does not measure time the way we do (v. 8), nor is His agenda the same as ours (v. 9). Rather than being untrustworthy in delaying His promises, the Lord is merciful, Peter argues. In His great love, He is patiently waiting to bring as many to salvation as possible before He returns, so that none might perish (v. 9). What some perceive to be a blatant failure on God's part (v. 4) is actually His immeasurable mercy at work (v. 9). Peter consequently exhorts us to patiently trust in God (vv. 14-15).

Although Peter is writing about the Lord's return, the distinction he makes between our time frame and God's are crucial. This means that if we are to persevere through the unexpected things until God answers our prayers, we might need to wait a lot longer than we would like to. Choosing to wait longer than we want to is never easy. It tests our faith in many ways. Abraham and Sarah's story show us why.

God promised Abraham that he would give him a son – an heir to inherit all the blessings God had bestowed on Abraham (Gen 15:4). This was a welcome promise from God because Abraham and his wife Sarah were childless (Gen 11:30; 15:2–3).

After receiving the promise, a number of years passed and nothing had happened on the baby front (Gen 16:2). Things were clearly not going as they had imagined. As they travelled along the narrow road of faith, we find them hatching their own plan. Abraham took Sarah's servant Hagar as a wife and had a child with her (v. 3). Their plan worked! Hagar conceived and gave birth to a son, Ishmael (v. 15). Abraham was 86 years old when Ishmael was born (v. 16).

But God was not satisfied with Abraham and Sarah's plan. He again visits Abraham and reiterates His promise to bless his barren wife Sarah with a son (Gen 17:16). Many years have now passed since God first promised them a son (Gen 15:4). This means that Abraham and Sarah are now even older, further reducing the likelihood of conception (Gen 17:17). Perhaps it was this awareness that caused Abraham to beseech God to accept Ishmael as his heir (v. 18)!

Nevertheless, God's purpose was fixed. His covenant would be established with the son He would give to barren Sarah and not with Hagar's son Ishmael (v.19). So, Abraham and Sarah were back to *waiting* for God, albeit perhaps reluctantly.

Finally, when Abraham was 100 years old, God fulfils His promise and Sarah gives birth to the promised Isaac (Gen 21:5). If Ishmael was born when Abraham was 86 and Isaac when he was 100, then Abraham and Sarah had to wait another 14 years before God fulfilled His promise. They had to wait a long time for Isaac.

God's promise birthed an expectation of fulfilment in Abraham and Sarah that differed vastly from God's timing. They received the promise and began waiting in faith for its fulfilment. But at some point, the waiting period extended beyond their initial expectation and we find them beginning to doubt God's promise and whether it even included Sarah[17], hence their Hagar plan (Gen 16:2).

Abraham and Sarah's story uncover our commonality in the struggle of patient faith – our tendency to filter God's promises through our *own* expectations. God's timing and theirs were clearly misaligned. When God took too long, they began searching for reasons for the imagined delay. This searching is ultimately what gave way to their resulting doubts and scheming.

We pass the interval between God's promise and its fulfilment by way of patient perseverance (Heb 6:12). For Abraham and Sarah, this interval was a long, seemingly endless road. Imagine the scene with me.

Every day they woke up to walk the same road, putting one foot of faith in front of the other, as they headed towards God's promise. The scenery seemed the same along this road, but every time they saw a bend up ahead, they wondered if they might be coming into His promise. When they did finally turn the corner, there was just another stretch of the same old road.

It was a road they now labelled "the waiting road" and it was becoming a rather tedious journey.

Each month brought with it the renewed hope that Sarah might fall pregnant, but each went by with them facing the same disappointment. Month in and month out, there was still no son and the joy of God's once welcome promise now began to fade.

The months ran into years and years into decades and still, they walked the same mundane road with God. They were growing weary of this process, weary of putting one foot of faith in front of the other. It was taking too long. They were growing tired of waiting, tired of the dot God had them in. Here they were sorely tempted to rename the road "the road to nowhere". They were impatient in their faith and growing more desperate for a son. These proved a lethal combination because one morning they woke up and decided that they would no longer wait for God. They would abandon this very long road of faith and forge their own path to surer success.

Abraham and Sarah effectively joined their own dots and drew a line that got them to the point of their desire – a son. But God was not satisfied with the outcome (Gen 17:21). As a result, God lead them into a time of recovery and brought them back to His original plan: Isaac, the son of God's promise, and the one He would establish His covenant with.

Much like Abraham and Sarah, we too find it difficult to stay on the path of perseverance in these in-between times because here we discover that we must wait longer than we want to. And because we don't know how long that will be, our faith is tested. For we too must stay on "the waiting road" of God's promises, putting one foot of faith in front of the other, even when we are growing frustrated with the delays and weariness of the journey.

When Abraham and Sarah ran out of patience and chose to leave the way of perseverance, they created a messy situation that brought them all grief. Their impatience might have brought them the long yearned-for son, but it also triggered a chain of strife in their home. Sarah was now upset with Abraham (Gen 16:5) because she and Hagar were continually fighting (v. 6). This conflict led to Sarah and Abraham evicting Hagar and Ishmael (Gen 21:8). Now that I think of it, their mess would make a great soap opera!

Abraham and Sarah aren't alone in this department. I've created some impatient messes of my own, as I'm sure you have, too. How many times do we make our own way because whatever we're waiting for, it's taking too long and we want it *now*? How many times have we allowed impatience to stir up doubt and unbelief concerning God's promises?

Abraham and Sarah's story highlights the prerequisite for realising God's promises – patience. We can't persevere through the interval between the promise and its fulfilment if we're impatient. Impatience tells us to hurry up and make a plan, to use what we can and improvise. You need relief and you need it now, so do something quick!

The assumption that we can in some way rush God is a futile one. God has a set time for everything; nothing He does is haphazard: "There is a time for everything, and a season for every activity under the heavens" (Eccl 3:1 NIV).

Sometimes God will let us know how long the wait will be. He told the Jewish exiles that He had set a period of 70 years for their captivity in Babylon (Jer 25:11–12; 29:10; 14). Even after all of Abraham and Sarah's shenanigans, God does in fact tell them when He is about to act: "Then one of them said, 'I will surely return to you about this time next year, and Sarah your wife will have a son'" (Gen 18:10 NIV).

But at other times, He doesn't let us know how long the wait will be. When the disciples asked Jesus for details about the time of His return, He replied: "But about that day or hour no one knows, not even the angels in heaven, nor the Son, but only the Father" (Matt 24:36 NIV).

Nevertheless, we're all called to wait patiently for God to fulfil His promises (Heb 6:12). We either wait for God or we don't. There is no midpoint. If we bail out of perseverance, we'll end up making our own way. We'll draw our own messy lines, the way Abraham and Sarah did with Ishmael.

Impatience erodes our faith in God. Whenever we're tempted to become impatient, we're allowing the enemy to stir up doubt in God's promises and we're in danger of abandoning our trust in God.

There's no other way to bridge the gap between God's promises and their fulfilment except by patient perseverance. In the first instance, waiting on God for our daily strength (Isa 40:31; Ps 27:14) and in the second, waiting for God to act on our behalf (Prov 20:22; Isa 30:18; Zeph 3:8).

Chapter 15:

CHOOSE TO BE FLEXIBLE

"And we know that in all things God works for the good of those who love him,who have been called according to his purpose."

(Rom 8:28 NIV)

Abraham and Sarah's story highlights another important truth. The fulfilment of God's promises in our lives rarely works out in the way we expected. His ways are higher than our ways (Isa 55:8). The time frame and the way in which God fulfilled His promise to give Abraham and Sarah a son didn't in any way match their expectations.

If we are to stay on the road of perseverance, we must learn to keep adjusting our expectations. I place the emphasis on us and not on God because the problem is never with God. He is perfect. His works and ways are perfect (Deut 32:4; 2 Sam 22:31). He is never late and never wrong in the way He deals with us – even in the midst of the unexpected things. He is not to blame for the consequences of sin (Mark 10:18). This is our holy and loving God's true nature.

Any adjustments that need to be made to expectations are always on our end, never His. If it doesn't happen within our time frame, then we must readjust our expectations, reset and wait a little longer. A delay in breakthrough necessitates a longer waiting period – the call of the Holy Spirit to keep persevering.

If God's answer comes in an unexpected way, then we must adjust our expectations of how we think it should have worked out and trust Him in the way it did, even when we are disappointed with the result. A different outcome to the one we anticipated is God's invitation to us to measure answered prayer differently.

I received such an invitation just recently. My elderly parents owned a plot of land that we'd been trying to sell for them for 20 years. It seems a long time to sell a piece of land, but this was no ordinary piece of land. It was situated in a desirable outlying area that was beginning to develop. As a result, my parents began to receive generous offers from different developers. Yet each time an offer was made, the deal would fall through.

Every successive offer indicated that the value of the land was increasing. We were hopeful of a good outcome. But even though the offers kept coming, for some reason they kept falling through. As the years passed, the situation became more dire. My parents were without income because their retirement capital was tied up in that property.

As their daughter, I wanted them to get the best price for their land. It was a goal I relentlessly pursued in prayer, faith and action as I sought to help them. In the meantime, my elderly parents were still living on the land and it was costing Stuart and I a lot of money to maintain. The need for God's intervention was significant.

Then they received a very good offer from a reputable developer. The developer wanted an entire parcel of land and made offers to a number of my parents' neighbours. They all accepted the offer, except for one neighbour who wanted more money than the land was worth. As a result, we lost the deal. The developer went ahead with their plans and bought all the other stands, but left our difficult neighbour and my parents' plot out of the development.

After this, there were other offers, but none that stuck. During this time, I tried to secure some sort of income for my parents. The land was situated on a busy road, so I met with advertising companies to place billboards on the land. This would secure a monthly income for my parents. These companies were keen, but in the due diligence process, we discovered that the boards would have to be set too far from the road to be seen. It was an anomaly as there were massive billboards all along this road, but for some reason our property was restricted. It didn't make any sense and further investigation lead only to one dead end after another.

Property agents came and went. Another ten years passed until we received another good offer, again by a reputable developer. We accepted the offer, but the sale process was laborious. A number of suspensive conditions had to be met. The developer needed to gain approvals for their plans to ensure a return on their investment.

Almost two years into this process, at the very last approval, the deal again fell through. The final suspensive condition couldn't be fulfilled for reasons beyond our or the buyer's control. The council regulations kept changing according to the rapid development of the area. Whoever rezoned the land for development would lose the existing property access onto the busy road. They would have to build a new access road through a number of our neighbours' properties. This was a massive access process that the council refused to assist with. The developer wanted the land specifically because of its access to the busy road.

After this, I tried everything. I met with traffic engineers to understand the access issues and town planners about rezoning and possible alternatives. I even called a meeting with some neighbours to encourage them to participate in a joint effort regarding an access road. They all had access to that same busy road and faced the same issue. Absolutely nothing worked. There seemed to be no way forward without significant financial outlay and even then, getting our neighbours to contribute some of their land for an access road would be an Everest to climb with little chance of success.

We waited another seven years during which we received more offers, none of which succeeded in a sale. In desperation, we decided to lease an unused part of the property to a trailer-hire business for a small monthly rental. It wasn't much, but it was something. My parents kept living in their house on the property. It worked well for a while until criminals broke in one night. It was month-end and they assumed that my parents had money in the house. For hours, the burglars held my niece and her boyfriend hostage. They stabbed and beat them, while they made their way through the house, stealing things of value. It was a traumatic ordeal for our family.

This security risk was too high for my parents to continue leasing the property, so we gave notice to the trailer-hire company and found ourselves back at square one. Waiting. And this is only half of what we went through with this property. Finally, at the end of 2022, we sold the land – praise God!

But here's the thing: it didn't work out as we expected it to. We sold it for far less than we were ever offered previously. The outcome looked completely different to what we'd imagined.

I was deeply disappointed. Much fasting, prayer and perseverance had gone into the sale of this land to secure financial provision for my parents in their retirement. It seemed as if all my efforts had been wasted. If we'd known in the beginning that we would sell the land for such a small amount, we could have sold it 100 times over during the 20-year period. We could have saved ourselves a lot of unnecessary time and effort.

During this trial, as we faced delay after delay, I recognised that I was being called to perseverance. I understood that I was being called to wait a little longer in faith. I even shared about this when I was asked to write about hope for our women's ministry:

> I have been trusting God to sell a piece of land for 15 years and I am still waiting in perseverance for Him to bring me the buyer – in His time. I need this money to take care of my ageing parents who don't have a pension. This land is their pension and time is of the essence as they are approaching their late seventies. I don't know how long I will have to wait until it is His time, but one thing I do know: to realise my breakthrough, I must stay anchored to the many precious promises He has given me over the years for this land and stay in faith. If I am to remain steadfast in my faith – immovable – I have to keep my heart full of hope, even though every circumstance and situation regarding this land has so far led to a dead end.

It was by God's grace alone that I managed to hold on in faith, believing that He would lead us to a successful sale. But what really challenged me was coming to grips with the final outcome because it looked completely different to what I had imagined.

It felt as if I had failed my parents and, in some ways, like I'd even failed God. Maybe there was something else I could have done? It was a trying time. When I remember everything we went through, the way it worked out still perplexes me.

In my mind, I had a picture of what the outcome would look like. This picture was shaped by the buzz of development interest in the property. Yes, there were ebbs and flows, but nevertheless, the offers kept coming over the years. The picture I'd formed was fuelling my expectation about reaching a particular outcome. When the property eventually sold and the outcome looked nothing like the picture in my mind, my disappointment was acute.

In the depths of my discouragement and despair, I sought God with fresh tears. And it was here that He began to gently, but surely, nudge me towards a different perspective. I had measured the sale of the property by my own expectation and He was inviting me to see it differently. For the property was sold and my elderly parents could now have a pension – I could praise God for this answered prayer! It might not have happened the way I expected it to, but nevertheless, it was done.

I wish I could tell you that making these necessary adjustments was an easy spiritual process. That it was easy to just shift my perspective and quickly remeasure the way God had answered my prayers on this matter. But it wasn't easy. After holding onto an anticipated outcome for 20 years, it was extremely difficult to reconcile my unmet expectations. During this process with the Lord, I discovered that the power of my expectation was much stronger than I'd realised. It took me a while to discern that my expectation (my imagined outcome for the situation) was leading my trust in God, rather than the other way around. This explained why I was so disappointed with the outcome. My faith was clouded by a specific desired outcome and, at some point, this expectation eclipsed my belief that God would work it out as He saw fit.

The two disciples whom Jesus met on the road to Emmaus grappled with a similar issue after Jesus' unexpected death (Luke 24:13). They were perplexed and discouraged by what had recently happened in Jerusalem. Jesus had just been crucified and they'd lost their hope in Israel's redemption (v. 21). These disciples had formed an expectation of what that would look like and Jesus dying was in none of these imagined scenarios.

Their disappointment weighed heavily on them (Luke 24:17). In the midst of their dejection, Jesus draws alongside them and asks them what has happened. Not knowing that they were talking with the resurrected Lord, they began to fill Him in. Imagine the conversation with me (See Luke 24). Jesus of Nazareth, whom we believed was the One who would rescue Israel, was suddenly sentenced to death by the Jewish rulers and crucified. Furthermore, it's the third day and a crazy thing happened this morning. Some of the women in our group went to His tomb and found it empty. But that's not all, even more bizarre, they claim they were met by angels who told them that Jesus has risen from the dead. So, some of us went to check it out and found it to be true – His body is not there!

The Lord's reply to these disciples is profound. He tells them that His suffering was necessary (Luke 24:26). They didn't see it that way. They felt their hopes had been dashed. They saw it as unmet expectations, even empty promises, because the Lord was dead. What good was the Lord's death in achieving Israel's redemption? But Jesus interprets the Scriptures for them to show them how His death and resurrection were indeed necessary (v. 27).

Notice how Jesus links their disappointment to unbelief: "And he said to them, 'O foolish ones, and slow of heart to believe all that the prophets have spoken!'" (Luke 24:25 ESV). At first glance, it seems an unfair correlation, particularly in light of their pain and confusion over recent events. But by doing so, the Lord points to the root issue in their hearts. Their expected outcome – their picture as to how Jesus should redeem Israel – was greater than their belief that God would work it out as He saw fit.

Jesus shows these disciples that their eyes of faith were blinded by the expectation they'd fashioned. They couldn't see past their disappointments to discover the truth of God's purposes. It's only as Jesus enables them to look through a different lens that they discover the truth of why His suffering was all necessary. But first they had to lay down their own expectations and disappointments.

If we are to stay on the path of perseverance, so must we. We too must put down our expectations of how we think things ought to be or should have worked out and trust God to work it out according to His will (Matt 6:10). His infinite ways always trump our finite expectations. As I journeyed with Jesus through my own disappointment, His daily grace enabled me, bit by bit, to make the necessary faith adjustments. I was able to reframe my expectations about the sale of my parents' property according to His unfailing faithfulness and goodness. Once again, I yielded to, "Your will be done" (Matt 6:10b ESV).

Through this experience, my trust in Him has grown rather than waned. The Holy Spirit has taught me an important faith lesson: our expectations of how God will fulfil His promises in our lives must *always* remain subject to our unfailing trust in Him.

The way of perseverance is a journey of continual adjustments. If we fail to make them, we're at risk of choosing the way of pride. This form of pride assumes that we know better than God. It's a pride that exalts ourselves and our ways above God and His (Isa 55:8–9). If we assume that God got it wrong, let us down or failed us in some way, we reduce God and His unfailing Word (Isa 55:11) to a mere human experience. And from here we easily stumble into Job and his three friends' folly, as we presumptuously contest the incontestable ways of God (Job 11:7–9).

To trust God means we don't rely on our own understanding, but choose to submit all our ways to Him:

> Trust God from the bottom of your heart; don't try to figure out everything on your own. Listen for God's voice in everything you do, everywhere you go; he's the one who will keep you on track. Don't assume that you know it all (Prov 3:5–7 MSG).

One more thing. Notice that Jesus came to walk alongside the disciples in their hurt confusion (Luke 24:15). The Lord yearns to draw close to us and help us with our disappointments. He wanted them to see how His suffering was necessary and restore their faith in Him (vv. 25–27). The Lord longs to do the same for us in our places of disappointment.

Sometimes our disillusionment is so great that we don't even recognise that Jesus is there with us (Luke 24:16). But if we will invite Him in, He will help us process our disappointments like He did with the two disciples on the road to Emmaus.

About seven months after the sale of my parents' property, our church had a time of corporate prayer and fasting. Up until then, I'd been searching for external evidence of why the sale at the low price was necessary. It still made no sense to me. Now, in this place of consecration before Him, He turned my gaze inward to the unseen, but necessary work of His Spirit in my inner man.

There is no better way to tell you what the Lord said to me than to share what I wrote in my journal at the time:

> It was all necessary for enlargement on the inside – in your inner man where I dwell. There you will find the evidence of why it was all necessary. I have been enlarging your spiritual capacity and the evidence will be seen in the fruit I will bear through you in this coming season.

Earlier we saw how Peter noted the vast difference between our face-value assumptions and God's agenda (2 Pet 3:9). We reduce our own faith when we look only to our outward lives and rate God according to which prayer/promise He has or hasn't answered/fulfilled. This reckoning of the Almighty God's faithfulness is not only unwise, but completely skewed. For there is another part to our lives – our hidden, inner life.

Don't get me wrong. I'm not saying that God isn't interested in meeting our outward needs. He most definitely is:

> So do not worry, saying, "What shall we eat?" or "What shall we drink?" or "What shall we wear?" For the pagans run after all these things, and your heavenly Father knows that you need them. But seek first his kingdom and his righteousness, and all these things will be given to you as well (Matt 6:31-33 NIV).

What I'm saying is that He is also fully invested in developing our inner life:

> If there is a natural body, there is also a spiritual body. So it is written: "The first man Adam became a living being"; the last Adam, a life-giving spirit. The spiritual did not come first, but

> the natural, and after that the spiritual. The first man was of the dust of the earth; the second man is of heaven. As was the earthly man, so are those who are of the earth; and as is the heavenly man, so also are those who are of heaven. And just as we have borne the image of the earthly man, so shall we bear the image of the heavenly man (1 Cor 15:44b–49 NIV).

Sometimes we'll only find the reasons for why it was all necessary in God's inner dealings with our hearts. His priority is always to bring us to spiritual maturity (Rom 8:29). This priority is greater than our expectations and time frames for attaining outward things.

The seen things tend to be *our* priority, but God's priority is often His unseen work to transform us, by His Spirit, into the very image of Jesus Christ (John 17:26; 1 Cor 15:49; Eph 4:24). If waiting a long time and persevering through difficulties allows God to enhance Christ's likeness in us, then it is something we should welcome and endure by His grace.

Which do we prize the most – when God does something outwardly, intervening in our circumstances, or when He does something hidden in us that will bring Him glory and bear fruit for eternity?

Let's not forget that God delights in answering our prayers (John 16:23–27; Isa 65:24). However, we should also remember that His work to bring us to spiritual maturity never stops. Every delay to the external answers we're seeking presents us with an opportunity to tune into the work He is also busy doing in our inner lives to bring us to maturity in Christ.

If we let our finite expectations lead our faith, there is only one destination – disillusionment. When we let God lead our faith, our expectations always remain subject to His unfailing goodness and faithfulness. In this way, we're able to make adjustments to continue trusting in the Alpha and Omega (Rev 22:13).

Chapter 16:

CHOOSE TO ENDURE HARDSHIP

"For you have need of endurance,
so that when you have done the will of God,
you may receive what is promised."
(Heb 10:36 ESV)

Our decision to trust God through the unexpected things leads us to only one end – we "have need of endurance" (Heb 10:36 ESV).

Choosing the more difficult option of faith and waiting longer than we expected means we will have to endure some difficult seasons. Waiting for God to act on our behalf means we must persevere through the unexpected season we find ourselves in.

A decision to trust God is ultimately a resolution to endure hardship while we wait for breakthrough. It's a determination to hang in there, even when the going gets tough. It means we hold fast to the Lord and cultivate a steadfast faith that can't be moved by our surrounding circumstances.

In 2017, I watched a tennis match that demonstrates this type of tenacity. It was the women's French Open final between the 3rd seed Simona Halep and the 47th ranked and unseeded Jelena Ostapenko, who was only 20 years old.

Ostapenko was losing badly. She had lost the first set and was 0-3 games down in the second. At this stage, she was completely outmatched and it seemed as if it was going to be a quick and easy win for Halep. Normally, I lose interest when one player dominates the match like this, but I was drawn to the young Ostapenko who, despite losing horribly, was giving her all to every ball she faced. It almost seemed as if she was oblivious to the scoreboard and this grabbed my attention.

As the game progressed, I was completely enthralled with Ostapenko's resolve and found myself hoping against hope that she would manage to at least put some points on the board to avoid scoring nil in the second set. Some of her shots were truly dismal: a humiliating defeat seemed inevitable. Yet she would not relent!

Her resolve was palpable as she kept striking the ball with all her might in the hopes that she would land a winner. Even in the face of obvious defeat, she wouldn't allow herself to yield to it and stubbornly stuck to her strategy. It was truly amazing to watch her in action.

Every time she lost a point, she would glance up at her coach to show her immense frustration. And each time she was met with an understanding look that said, "Keep going – you can do this!" So, she kept on and tackled the next point.

Through her sheer dogged determination, she slowly started knocking her opponent back one resolute point at a time. It was hard to tell who was the most surprised at the points she started to win, Ostapenko or Halep. Regardless, she just kept on smashing each ball with unaffected tenacity.

The crowd got behind her and was cheering every point she managed to win. They too had become enamoured with this young player's fighting spirit. And slowly but surely, Ostapenko started clawing her way back into the match.

It seemed impossible for Ostapenko to win the second set, but at least she was starting to win a few games – the undesired donut score now averted. Eventually she knocked her opponent back to win the second set and more. Ostapenko's daring resolve took her all the way through the match to win the final! It was a victory that shocked everyone – perhaps even herself.

It was a captivating display of sheer determination. Ostapenko broke a number of records. She was the first Latvian to win the title and the first unseeded champion since 1933[18]. What an achievement for this talented player! And yet what stood out the most was this young woman's tenacity. She pushed through the losses and the pressure she must have felt. She just kept swinging her racket, returning one ball at a time, in the hope that she would eventually land a winner. Her unrelenting perseverance has remained with me all these years.

I have often heard Grand Slam commentators say that it's the mental toughness of a player that inevitably pushes them ahead of their talented opponents. At a professional level, all players are exceptionally talented, but the victory usually goes to the one who has the fortitude to keep pushing through each challenge. For this reason, mental toughness is very much a part of the modern player's training.

The one who can absorb the intense pressures within a match and not allow them to negatively affect their game has an edge over their opponent. It's no wonder that the main court at Roland Garros displays this quote from its namesake, "Victory Belongs to the Most Tenacious."

As believers, we too need to develop this type of tenacity, a tenacity to endure the challenges of this match called life. We need to cultivate tenacious faith! Our faith should be strong enough to absorb the pressures of life and not to give up when the going gets tough. We shouldn't want to quit when the scoreboard is firmly against us. Even in the absence of breakthrough, our faith should be holding fast to the Lord in unrelenting trust.

Yes, we will lose some points and we might even be a set down and facing an inevitable thumping. But if you will look up into your player's box, you will see your coach sitting right there. His name is Jesus and He is your sole advantage in the midst of the all the chaos closing in on you. He hasn't taken His eyes off you – not once. He has seen every loss and felt your every hurt. He is there, in the thick of it with you. And right now, He knows exactly what you must do to keep standing firm in your faith. Just ask Him. Go and seek His precious face. He is ready to coach you in the midst of all the crushing pressures you face. The scoreboard might show you are on a hiding to nothing, but don't focus on that, dear beloved of God.

What matters is not the story the score is telling you right now; what matters is what your Heavenly Father has promised you in covenant faithfulness – if you will trust Him.

You might be down in games and reeling from the many losses, but in the end, you will win the match – Christ has secured this victory for you. Today, He invites you to endure in faith as you trust Him, for if you do, you will most assuredly inherit His immeasurable promises (Heb 10:36).

Tenacious faith absorbs the immense pressures of the unexpected things and remains steadfast. But this ability is not something we can manufacture. Rather, it is Christ within us. Christ is the power working within us, empowering us with the strength of His might to remain steadfast as we endure hardship (Eph 1:19; 3:7; 3:20–21; Luke 17:21; Col 1:29). He absorbs the full brunt of the pressure on our behalf, as He invites us to cast all our anxieties upon Him (1 Pet 5:7). It's only because Jesus is within us that we can take up a position of quiet trust and endure difficulties.

When we are facing insurmountable challenges, it helps to know that we don't have to scramble around for the strength we need to endure. It's a wonderful relief to know Christ will do it in and through us. His victory allows us to develop a steadfast and immovable faith (1 Cor 15:58).

Much like the determination displayed by Ostapenko, tenacious faith pushes through the losses and intense pressure of the unexpected things. It's a faith that takes one trusting step at a time, in the hope that the next one might be the one to bring us victory!

What does this type of resilient faith look like? We see it in action in the life of David. David was about 15 years old when the prophet Samuel anointed him Israel's next king to replace Saul[19] (1 Sam 16:1; 12–13). Yet David only became king much later at the age of 30 (2 Sam 5:4). And then he only reigned as the king of Judah, the southern part of Israel (2 Sam 2:4). He had to wait another seven-and-a-half years before he finally became king over all of Israel (2 Sam 5:3–5).

Through all these years of waiting for the fulfilment of God's promise, David had to endure many challenges. David didn't appoint himself as Israel's future king – he was chosen by God. It was a God-given destiny that would lead David through all sorts of unexpected difficulties – most of which were not his own doing. The dots that would ultimately connect him to his God-given destiny were marked by disappointment, distress, loss and adversity.

King Saul did not take kindly to being replaced (1 Sam 18). An unstable and insecure man, Saul initially played political games with David – at one moment, keeping David close to him and at others, hurling spears at him to kill him.

Seeking an alliance with David, Saul promised him the hand of his daughter Merab but then promptly gave her to another man (1 Sam 18:19). This must have hurt both David and Merab, particularly if they had formed a relationship ahead of their marriage. Again, David is promised another of Saul's daughters, Michal. But first he has to survive Saul's scheme to have him killed in battle while securing the bridal price. To earn the hand of Michal, David has to kill 100 Philistines, Israel's arch-enemy (1 Sam 18:25). David takes Saul at his word, knowing full well that he can't be trusted.

Later Saul gave up the pretence of liking David and launched an all-out offensive to eliminate him (1 Sam 18:10; 19:2). It was a move that upended David's life, causing him to live on the run and in constant hiding (1 Sam 19:18–20). Let's take a closer look at some of the unexpected things David had to persevere through during this time.

David was forced to abandon his wife and home (1 Sam 19:11–13). He had to be careful not to be seen in public, as he did not know whom he could trust (1 Sam 22:9–10; 23:19). He lived like a fugitive and yet was blameless (1 Sam 20:1). His only crime was that God had chosen him to be Israel's next king and Saul hated him for it.

A wanted man, David resorted to living in fields and caves in an attempt to stay alive (1 Sam 20:5; 22:1). And when Saul's vendetta intensified, David was no longer safe and had to go into exile in Philistia (1 Sam 21:13). This was not the safest place for David to be, having killed their champion Goliath (1 Sam 17) and having fought against them many times as the commander of Saul's army (1 Sam 18:5; 30).

Not only was David's life in continual danger, but also the lives of all who were connected to him. His entire family had to leave their homes and go into exile with him (1 Sam 22:1–3). Anyone that had contact with David was immediately seen as an enemy of Saul and was in danger of losing their life. At one time, Saul slaughtered an entire village of priests and their families, not even sparing the livestock because he suspected one of them, Ahimelek, might have helped David escape (1 Sam 22:18–19). Saul's vendetta against David led to the senseless deaths of many innocent people and David felt these losses keenly (1 Sam 22:22).

Saul put David through untold suffering. Yet, through it all, we find that David never retaliated with vengeance. Instead, he often made difficult choices, even when he knew they would invariably prolong his own suffering. David chose the way of enduring faith. And he did so repeatedly.

He made the difficult choice to respect Saul as Israel's king, rather than mount a rebellion against him. He made the difficult choice to suffer the painful separation from his wife, home and loved ones, rather than fight for his own justice (1 Sam 26:19). He chose not to harm Saul, even when the opportunity presented itself as a seemingly divine opportunity (1 Sam 24:4; 26:8). Remarkably, David even defends his murderous persecutor and prevents his men from killing him (1 Sam 24:7; 26:8–9).

He chose to go into exile in enemy territory, rather than retaliate (1 Sam 27:1). He chose to suffer many losses, while he waited patiently for God to intervene on his behalf.

These years of waiting were by no means easy for David. He lost his wife, home, friends, country and freedom. As if this weren't enough, he bore the pain of knowing that others had lost their lives because of Saul's feud against him (1 Sam 22:22).

But David didn't do it alone and he didn't do it in his own strength. The source of his enduring strength was his unrelenting trust in the Lord. He trusted God with his present circumstances as much as he trusted Him with his promised future (1 Sam 24:12; 26:24). A hunted man, he was often just a breath away from certain death (1 Sam 23:26–27). Yet again and again, we find David turning to God for help and direction in quiet trust (1 Sam 23:2; 10–11; 30:6–8). It was this unyielding trust in God that brought David through these tumultuous times and the many that he would later face as Israel's king.

In response to David's faith, God shows him His covenant faithfulness. As David endured, God delivered, protected and provided for him. He delivered David out of Saul's hand; none of Saul's attempts to kill him succeeded (1 Sam 23:4; 14; 26–28; 27:4). He protected David from the temptation of taking matters into his own hands and connecting his own dots (1 Sam 24:5–6; 25:39; 26:11).

God continually provided for David and those with him, leading them to places of refuge. While in exile, God gave them favour with the king of the Philistines, who even gave them the town of Ziklag to settle in (1 Sam 22:5; 12; 27:6). And when, in David's absence, the Amalekites destroyed Ziklag and captured all their wives and children, God again delivered David and his companions and helped them recover their loved ones (1 Sam 30).

We can clearly see the evidence of God's covenant faithfulness toward David. That's not to say that the path of endurance was easy for David. He suffered many losses along the way and each one brought him pain and sorrow. The attack at Ziklag is a particularly low point in David's life and deserves closer scrutiny.

Just prior to this incident, Achish, the king of Gath, is preparing to go to war against Israel. He asks David and his exiled men to accompany the Philistines to fight against Israel. David consents (1 Sam 28:1–2). But when David and his men prepare to attack, the Philistine commanders reject David's help. They are concerned that David and his men will turn on them in battle and fight for and not against Israel (1 Sam 29:4). As a result, King Achish sends David and his men back (1 Sam 29:7).

They make the three-day journey back to Ziklag (1 Sam 30:1), but on arrival discover that, in their absence, the Amalekites have attacked their hometown and captured all their loved ones (1 Sam 30:3). This loss was one that was painfully felt by David and his men: "Then David and the people who were with him raised their voices and wept until they had no more strength to weep" (1 Sam 30:4 ESV).

At another time, we see David openly expressing his pain when he realises he must leave his home, his family and his best friend Jonathan, Saul's son, for a life on the run:

> After the boy had gone, David got up from the south side of the stone and bowed down before Jonathan three times, with his face to the ground. Then they kissed each other and wept together—but David wept the most (1 Sam 20:41 NIV).

David felt the pain and disappointment of the unexpected things he encountered. Yes, he endured. Yes, he had faith and trust in His God. And yes, God's covenant faithfulness toward him was unrelenting. But he also cried in the pain of it at times.

Feeling pain and disappointment is not a sign of mistrust in God. It's not a sign that God is not with us, fighting for us and working in us. David was full of faith in His God, yet David still expressed the pain of the losses he incurred along the way. And God never rebukes him for this! We can feel and express the pain of our circumstances and still possess tenacious faith. Again, David shows us how after the destruction of Ziklag:

> David was greatly distressed because the men were talking of stoning him; each one was bitter in spirit because of his sons and daughters. But David found strength in the Lord his God (1 Sam 30:6 NIV).

David took his pain to God. He runs to God for comfort and here he found the strength to keep moving forward. We see this in David's life throughout his journey to the throne. He seeks God and turns to Him for answers continually:

> ...and David inquired of the Lord, "Shall I pursue this raiding party? Will I overtake them?"
>
> "Pursue them," He answered. "You will certainly overtake them and succeed in the rescue" (1 Sam 30:8 NIV).

In the pain of Ziklag, David pauses to seek God's counsel. Notice that David doesn't allow his crisis to dictate his reaction. Rather, he turns to God in quiet trust and waits on Him for the way forward. It is a remarkable spiritual discipline in the life of David, one that's rewarded with God's faithful guidance and provision.

David and his men pursued the marauding Amalekites and, true to God's promise, they defeated them and recovered all their loved ones (1 Sam 30:18). By following God's lead through the unexpected things and by choosing to trust Him, David achieves victory and rescues those who were taken by the Amalekites. It's a victory that gives him and his weary men the strength to return to their razed town and begin the work of rebuilding it (1 Sam 30:26).

David's dot journey to the throne was still in process. He hadn't yet come to the place of fulfilment, but as he endured its hardships in quiet trust, God gave him many victories. The story of Ziklag is just one of these.

Every time David escapes Saul's clutches is a victory. Every time he finds a safe hiding place is a victory. Every time he encounters favour with the Philistines is a victory. Every time God shows him the way forward is a victory. Every time David turns to God in faith and trust is a victory!

Enduring in faith and trust through hardship is never easy. There is pain on this path and yes, some losses too. But it is also a path saturated with God's immeasurable covenant faithfulness. It's also the only path that leads us into His promises (Heb 10:36).

At one of David's lowest points in Ziklag, he had no idea that a fulfilment dot lay right around the corner. As David pursued the Amalekites to fight yet another demanding battle, he had no way of knowing that his Ziklag signalled the winds of change. These winds would soon clear the long-endured fog of his unexpected circumstances.

While facing one of his toughest leadership challenges, David didn't know that very soon events beyond his control (but firmly within the Lord's) would move him into his long-awaited breakthrough! This would be the first dot of many that would connect him to a brand-new season in which he would finally become king, first of Judah and then over a united Israel (2 Sam 2:4; 5:3).

David discovered early on that the source of his resilient faith was his unrelenting trust in God. It is why he could, with utter conviction, one day write:

> The Lord is my strength and my shield;
> in him my heart trusts, and I am helped;
> my heart exults, and with my song I give thanks to him.
> (Ps 28:7 ESV)

Early in his relationship with the Lord, David learned that it was this unrelenting trust that connected him to His ongoing help, provision and deliverance, which is why at another time he could emphatically state that it was the Lord, "who has redeemed my life out of every adversity" (2 Sam 4:9 ESV).

David had to make difficult choices again and again. He had to wait much longer than he'd probably have liked. He had to keep adjusting his expectations as he waited for God to act on his behalf. But he did these things knowing one thing with absolute certainty: it was the only way to realise God's promises. He tells us so in his own words in the many psalms he penned. Take a moment to reflect on this one with regard to his faith attitude in the midst of adversity:

> I will bless the Lord at all times;
> his praise shall continually be in my mouth.
> My soul makes its boast in the Lord;
> let the humble hear and be glad.
> Oh, magnify the Lord with me,
> and let us exalt his name together!

I sought the Lord, and he answered me
and delivered me from all my fears.
Those who look to him are radiant,
and their faces shall never be ashamed.
This poor man cried, and the Lord heard him
and saved him out of all his troubles.
The angel of the Lord encamps
around those who fear him, and delivers them.

Oh, taste and see that the Lord is good!
Blessed is the man who takes refuge in him!
Oh, fear the Lord, you his saints,
for those who fear him have no lack!

The young lions suffer want and hunger;
but those who seek the Lord lack no good thing.
Come, O children, listen to me;
I will teach you the fear of the Lord.
What man is there who desires life
and loves many days, that he may see good?
Keep your tongue from evil
and your lips from speaking deceit.
Turn away from evil and do good;
seek peace and pursue it.

The eyes of the Lord are toward the righteous
and his ears toward their cry.
The face of the Lord is against those who do evil,
to cut off the memory of them from the earth.
When the righteous cry for help, the Lord hears
and delivers them out of all their troubles.

The Lord is near to the broken-hearted
and saves the crushed in spirit.

Many are the afflictions of the righteous,
but the Lord delivers him out of them all.
He keeps all his bones;
not one of them is broken.
Affliction will slay the wicked,
and those who hate the righteous will be condemned.
The Lord redeems the life of his servants;
none of those who take refuge in him will be condemned (Psalm 34 ESV).

Chapter 17:

CHOOSE NOT TO QUIT

"By your endurance you will gain your lives."

(Luke 21:19 ESV)

I'm sure David felt tempted to give up on God's promises many times along the way. Perhaps he came closest to this quitting point in Ziklag. When the unexpected things keep rolling in like the unending waves of the ocean, the temptation to stop trusting God is real.

We know this from our own experiences. Having to persevere through hardship is often the place where turning to some sort of Egypt appears a really attractive alternative to quiet trust (Isa 30:1–3). Like the mythical sirens that waylaid many sailors, reliance on Egypt pulls at our weary souls, promising instant respite. Juxtaposed against it lies the path of quiet trust that stretches out before us with no end in sight.

Not knowing what lies ahead or how long we need to endure makes us scream, "This is too hard! I can't do this anymore! Does God not see my pain? This is unfair. I don't deserve this." Maybe David had similar words with God when he returned to find Ziklag destroyed and his family kidnapped.

If Ostapenko had given up when she was down the first set and losing 0–3 in the second, she could never have gone on to win the French Open, even though she had the talent and ability to do so. If David had quit at Ziklag, he wouldn't have gone on to recover all that was stolen from him. These seem obvious observations after the events, but when these two individuals were in the thick of their respective losses, making the choice to keep going was anything but the obvious choice to make.

Each disappointing dot on David's journey was also connected to the ultimate dot of fulfilment. And because David remained in faith and trust, God could use every difficult dot in his life to bring him there.

That day in Ziklag, as David wept to the point of exhaustion and averted a revolt against his leadership (1 Sam 30:4–6), he found solace in the familiar place of God's presence. It was only in this place that he could once again find the strength and grace to keep choosing the way of faith and trust.

It was just one more routine choice to continue trusting God, but unbeknown to David, that day would be the "one more" that would finally bring him to the threshold of his breakthrough.

It was a long-awaited outcome, but it came at an unexpected time for David. He might have expected it the first week after he had to flee from Saul. He might have felt then that he was ready to see God move on his behalf now. Or when that didn't happen, he might have expected it a few months later as a fugitive. He must have thought to himself that his situation certainly didn't line up with God's promise that he would be Israel's next king. Surely God must be getting ready to act soon?

When that didn't happen, he might have expected it after he refused to avenge himself and kill Saul when they both found themselves in a cave (1 Sam 24:3). He may have concluded that his act of righteousness would be rewarded by God giving him the breakthrough he so dearly desired. But it wasn't. David remained a hunted man and with each subsequent disappointment, he needed to choose to keep trusting God.

We don't know how many times David hoped that he was on the verge of a breakthrough. We can only guess based on our own experiences.

As we trust God for deliverance, we know at which climactic points in our journey we too have hoped for a much-anticipated breakthrough. And we expect it to happen then! We pray for it to happen then. We have faith for it to happen then. But when it doesn't happen straight away, it presents us with yet another invitation to keep trusting God – to keep persevering in faith. Like David in Ziklag, we never know when a routine choice could usher in our breakthrough!

In David's case, though, there was a distinction. Within a short space of time, David went from the lowest low of Ziklag to the highest high of king of Judah. It might have felt the same for the unseeded Ostapenko, who went from zero (literally) to hero in a few short hours. This is the nature of breakthrough – we finally come to a point, after countless decisions to keep trusting and believing in God, where we break through the fog of the unexpected things and come into the clearing of His precious promises!

Quitting comes at the cost of realising our desired destination. For Ostapenko, this was a shot at a championship title. For David, it was attaining the throne as king of Israel. They both understood that the short gains of immediate relief couldn't compare to the prize of victory. Would David have persevered through so much hardship if he believed otherwise?

Whatever instant relief we seek to reduce the pain of our crisis can never come close to what God accomplishes through them. David demonstrates this by making the daily choice to keep trusting God, no matter how dire his circumstances are. The apostle Paul also states that all the crushing, perplexing and despairing afflictions he endured were but a "light momentary affliction" in comparison to what God had prepared for him (2 Cor 4:17 ESV). And then there is Job, whose unrelenting faith in God through untold misery, led to him eventually receiving "twice as much as he had before" (Job 42:10 ESV).

David, Paul and Job received the rich reward of their persevering faith – but will we? This is a question we must answer for ourselves. All three of these men chose the path of endurance. Will we choose to endure hardship in quiet trust as they did?

Chapter 18:

CHOOSE TO BE THERE AT THE END

"For we have come to share in Christ, if indeed we hold our original confidence firm to the end"

(Heb 3:14 ESV)

Much depends on how we finish our race for Jesus. The above verse reminds us that we will share in our rich inheritance in Christ only if we hold on to the Lord all the way to the end. There is an "if" in this sentence that signals a condition. That condition is that our faith must make it all the way to the end.

The way we run our race for Jesus is of primary importance in the life of every believer. We should run it in a way that ensures we'll make it all the way to the finish line – with our faith still intact.

The handle of perseverance is not a nice-to-have, something to steady ourselves on when the unexpected happens. It's a necessity of our faith. It gets us to the finish line.

Perseverance is the fuel that will keep our faith moving forward with God. Running out of it will bring our faith to a standstill. We must not allow this to happen, for then we will not come through the fog of the unexpected things and into the clearing of His amazing promises.

How much fuel we have in the tank matters a great deal. When travelling a long distance by road, we must plan and ensure that we will have enough to get us to our destination. We even navigate our road trip along a route that has many petrol stations, so that we can stop and refuel along the way. We do this to avoid getting stuck on the side of the road.

The Lord doesn't want us to get stranded! He wants us to share in His very rich inheritance (Rom 8:17). We must equip ourselves with what we need to connect all our dots and make it to the end of our journey. Only then can we uncover the complete picture of our lives for His eternal glory.

Our capacity to endure hardship will determine how far we go with Jesus. Having a little fuel, a half-full tank, is not enough to see us through this long journey.

Rather, we must make provision for this faith journey. We must regularly refill our tank to ensure that we always have enough to keep moving forward with God, right up to the finish line. Our tank must remain full otherwise, His promises will remain unfulfilled in our lives. This would be a great tragedy in light of all He has done to secure victory for us (Eph 1:7–9).

How disappointing it would be for us to start our race for Jesus well, continue on the path of faith, only to run out of perseverance at the last moment. What agony this would be! The Lord tells us this in His parable of the ten virgins:

> Then the kingdom of heaven will be like ten virgins who took their lamps and went to meet the bridegroom. Five of them were foolish, and five were wise. For when the foolish took their lamps, they took no oil with them, but the wise took flasks of oil with their lamps. As the bridegroom was delayed, they all became drowsy and slept. But at midnight there was a cry, 'Here is the bridegroom! Come out to meet him.' Then all those virgins rose and trimmed their lamps. And the foolish said to the wise, 'Give us some of your oil, for our lamps are going out.' But the wise answered, saying, 'Since there will not be enough for us

> and for you, go rather to the dealers and buy for yourselves.' And while they were going to buy, the bridegroom came, and those who were ready went in with him to the marriage feast, and the door was shut. Afterward the other virgins came also, saying, 'Lord, lord, open to us.' But he answered, 'Truly, I say to you, I do not know you.' Watch therefore, for you know neither the day nor the hour (Matt 25:1–13 ESV).

In this story, Jesus is the bridegroom and the virgins represent the believers who are eagerly awaiting His return (Rev 19:7; 21:2). The virgins (believers) are waiting in faith for His imminent return, which is a fulfilment of one of His promises:

> In my Father's house are many rooms. If it were not so, would I have told you that I go to prepare a place for you? And if I go and prepare a place for you, I will come again and will take you to myself, that where I am you may be also (John 14:2–3 ESV).

But for some reason, the bridegroom is delayed in His coming and the waiting period is extended. In other words, these ten virgins had chosen the way of faith and are on the path of perseverance, waiting for the fulfilment of God's promises. But it's taking a lot longer than they thought it would.

Five of them are wise and prepared themselves to wait as long as it took for the bridegroom's promised return. They made sure that they had an extra flask of oil, so that they could keep refuelling their lamps (v. 3). This is true wisdom. The others are unprepared for any type of delays – a decision the Lord called foolish because of its costly consequences. These five ill-equipped virgins do not enter His kingdom.

There are a number of similarities among this group of believers that are important for us to note. All ten virgins started out the same way. They were all invited to wait for the bridegroom's coming and were equipped with what they needed; each one had a lamp and access to the oil needed to fuel it (v. 1). They all had to wait for the same length of time and all succumbed to some degree of weariness (v. 5). They also all heard the call of His arrival (v. 6). But only five were still there to welcome the bridegroom when He finally arrived and only they could enter His kingdom (v. 10).

This parable contains an important lesson on endurance. In it, the Lord places believers into two categories: those who are prepared to make it all the way to the end and inherit all His promises, and those who don't.

The problem was not how they all began. The problem was how they all ended. When the bridegroom finally returned, some were ready to welcome Him and some weren't. The wise virgins had one advantage that distinguished them from the others – they took extra oil. They'd made provision beforehand for the waiting.

In their careful preparation, we glimpse a resolve in these believers. They weren't going to take any chances and somehow miss His arrival. They'd do whatever it took to ensure that they could keep their lamps burning until He returned. These five wise virgins had tenacious faith, the kind that endures all the way to the end.

Let's just take note that this is an extremely high drop-out rate of 50%! Could it be that half of all Christians on earth might not welcome Jesus when He finally returns? Are half of us not preparing our faith to ensure we endure to the end? I pray it isn't so! But here the Lord shows us that as many as half did not make it to the finish line (and into His kingdom) because they lacked the vital element of a prepared faith. That preparedness was found in the extra oil: it was the element that allowed the five wise virgins to still be there at the end.

Are we wise or foolish believers? We don't know the day or the hour of Christ's second coming. Nor when the fog of our circumstances will clear. What we do know is that in Him, our breakthrough is a certainty. But we need the oil of endurance. We need to be like the five wise virgins and be prepared to wait and persevere for as long as it takes to inherit His faithful promises.

The delay was the undoing of half the virgins. The delay revealed what was lacking in their preparations to meet the bridegroom. At the moment they needed it most, they lacked enough oil. It was a costly error! It meant that they didn't realise the fulfilment of His long-awaited promise (John 14:2–3). Oh, what agony! To make it so close, only to fall short at the end.

Will the delays in reaching our fulfilment dot be our undoing? Will the waiting period reveal what is lacking in our preparations to keep enduring right up until the end? God has already guaranteed His promises:

> People swear by someone greater than themselves, and the oath confirms what is said and puts an end to all argument. Because God wanted to make the unchanging nature of his purpose very clear to the heirs of what was promised, he confirmed it with an oath. God did this so that, by two unchangeable things in which it is impossible for God to lie, we who have fled to take hold of the hope set before us may be greatly encouraged (Hebrews 6:16–18 NIV).

We can have full confidence that God will do what He has promised (Rom 8:17). But coming into these promises requires perseverance. Perseverance is the essential oil that keeps our faith lamps lit. It is the key ingredient that ensures we are still there when God shows up with breakthrough in our unexpected circumstances.

We all need our own oil of endurance. I can't give you my oil. I can't endure your hardship for you, just as I can't secure your salvation (Phil 2:12). We all need to prepare our own faith with the oil of endurance for the race that is set before us (Heb 12:1).

The five wise virgins weren't being mean-spirited by not sharing their oil with the foolish virgins. They only had enough oil to fuel their own lamps (v. 9). Here, the Lord puts the responsibility firmly on every believer to ensure that they secure enough oil for themselves. Our personal spiritual development is our responsibility (Phil 2:12). It cannot be outsourced to another (Matt 25:9).

The good news is that we can all be like the five wise virgins. We can choose to equip our faith to endure until the end. We're well able to endure any difficulty because of what Jesus Christ has done for us through His death, resurrection and ascension: "No, in all these things we are more than conquerors through him who loved us" (Rom 8:37 NIV).

God has given us "very great and precious promises" (2 Pet 1:4 NIV). In order to receive them, we must add perseverance to our faith (2 Pet 1:6). And then we must keep developing our ability to persevere through hardship and adversity (2 Pet 1:8).

We don't just need the oil of perseverance – we need *extra* oil. The five unwise virgins had oil. They just didn't have enough to see them through any delays. We need to be like rally car drivers who participate in cross-continent events. They know that they'll need to pass through remote areas en route to the finish line and they prepare accordingly. They build in contingency, taking extra fuel and supplies to ensure that they'll have enough to get them through those isolated areas.

We need to build in contingency. Preparing our faith for all eventualities is particularly important when it comes to the unexpected things. It's why we need the extra capacity to stay the course and endure through hardship. The five wise virgins had built in contingency.

So how do we grow in perseverance? Where do we find this much-needed stamina for our dot journey in Christ? James tells us:

> Consider it pure joy, my brothers and sisters, whenever you face trials of many kinds, because you know that the testing of your faith produces perseverance. Let perseverance finish its work so that you may be mature and complete, not lacking anything (Jas 1:2-4 NIV).

Perseverance is a product of the testing of our faith. Now let me ask you something: when is your faith most tested? Is it during the good times, when all is plain sailing and we have peace on all our borders, so to speak (1 Kings 4:24)? Or is it when we meet the unexpected things?

The unexpected things ask some big questions of our faith and test our trust in a loving, faithful God. When storms hit our lives, all our beliefs are tested. Is God here right now (Josh 1:5)? Does He see what's happening to me and does He really care (Matt 7:9; 10:30)? Numerous similar questions gnaw at our faith as we wonder if we'll ever make it through. And every time there is a delay in realising what we're hoping for, our faith is again tested.

But this is where we gain perseverance. We grow in perseverance, the indispensable fuel of our faith, when our faith is tested (Jas 1:3). We increase our capacity to endure as we endure. We can't develop in perseverance without having to persevere through something.

THE SINE QUA NON

Perseverance is a necessity of life. Most of what we do on a daily basis requires effort and determination to accomplish. Very little in this life is simple. We'll always be dealing with some kind of difficulty and often just as we finish dealing with one, another is hot on its heels. The normal rhythms of life demand constant effort and, at times, even struggle.

Achieving the many responsibilities of life requires perseverance. In other words, perseverance is the *sine qua non** of life. We know that if we quit halfway through something, we'll never realise its completion. We even set goals in various aspects of our lives to help us stay on course. We set career goals, health goals, financial goals and relationship goals.

In these things, we easily accept and understand the role of perseverance and are willing to embrace its importance in reaching our objective. We know that if we don't endure to the end, we simply won't realise our goals.

However, when it comes to applying this same principle to our spiritual lives, we resist. We don't see perseverance as a necessity, but more as a failure on God's part.

If His promise hasn't yet come to pass, it tends to be because God hasn't come through for us, whereas in reality, it might simply be because we haven't persevered long enough. We wouldn't form this type of conclusion in any other area of our lives. We know that if we drop out of university, we won't graduate or that if we give up on our diet, we won't lose weight.

* *Sine qua non* is a Latin phrase which means an essential condition.

Perseverance is also a necessity in our spiritual lives, as unpopular as this notion might be. As disciples of Christ, we have been given spiritual goals. We are all called to grow up and become mature men and women in Christ (Eph 4:15–16). To this end, we should be developing and maintaining the various spiritual disciplines required to get us there.

Perseverance is a spiritual discipline. It is the *sine qua non* of our faith. By it, we position ourselves for uninterrupted cooperation with our partner, the Holy Spirit. From here, He can lead us safely through the fog of the unexpected things.

The seas of life are never plain sailing. Frightening storms do suddenly appear – just as abruptly as the one Jesus and His disciples encountered crossing the lake of Gennesaret (Matt 8:23–27). Storms will surely come, but we are fully equipped to overcome them because of the victory Christ has won for us (John 16:33; 1 John 5:4).

We must train ourselves to persevere in faith through the unexpected things if we are to connect all our dots. To give up is to surrender our God-given destiny.

Chapter 19:

PERSONAL REFLECTION

Succumb or Overcome?

"And let us not grow weary of doing good,
for in due season we will reap, if we do not give up."
(Gal 6:9 ESV)

When we meet the unexpected things, we have two faith choices: succumb or overcome. We either succumb under the weight of difficulty or we overcome it by our faith. The Lord wants us to overcome and He's made full provision for us to do just that.

Tenacious faith must be developed. By regularly making the choices outlined in this chapter we allow the Spirit to increase our capacity to persevere.

A large portion of our journey is still unseen. All we can see is the present. Today our faith needs endurance, so that we can patiently wait for the fulfilment of God's promises (Rom 8:25). For as long as we have today, we need to continually refill our tanks with the much-needed fuel of perseverance.

Putting It Into Practice: Handle of Perseverance

Spiritual Insight: Perseverance is the fuel that keeps my faith moving forward with God all the way to the end.

1. Perseverance is a necessity of faith. What is your reaction to this statement? What type of response does it trigger in you and why?

2. Egypt represents anything that we turn to that replaces our reliance on God.

a) What are some of the Egypt's you have turned to when facing hardship? List at least three.

b) Read Isaiah 30:15–17 and Proverbs 5:5–6. What can you do to move away from turning to these things and instead build greater trust in Almighty God?

3. Read Joshua 8:1–29. In your journey with God, what has He faithfully led you through?

4. Read Daniel 6:1–10. Daniel chose the more difficult option when he continued to pray to God even though it was forbidden. What are some of the difficult choices you are making now as a disciple of Jesus?

5. When standing in line, how many minutes is too long for you to wait before you become irritable?

a) What does this tell you about your natural tendency when it comes to waiting for God's promises to be fulfilled?

b) Read Ecclesiastes 3:1 and Psalm 27:13–14. What do you think it means to wait for the Lord?

6. Think of a prayer request you have right now. Write out your expected outcome to this prayer request. In other words, when God answers it, what do you think it will look like?

7. Read Luke 24:12–35. The two disciples had an expectation of what Jesus should have done for them. Jesus draws alongside them and helps them work through their unmet expectations. Discuss what it means to always keep our expectations of God subject to our unfailing trust in Him?

8. Read 2 Corinthians 11:24–28 and Acts 14:19–22. What does Acts 14:20–22 tell you about how Paul viewed the unexpected things of this life?

a) List three actions Paul took after his severe beating.

b) In your personal journey with Christ, what does Acts 14:22 mean to you?

9. Read Ephesians 3:14–21. Why is it possible for us to endure hardships?

10. List four ways you can turn the pressure of the unexpected things into opportunities to build tenacious faith. As you formulate your answers, consider David's example in his journey to the throne as Israel's king.

11. In the past, how have delays to breakthrough and answered prayer been the undoing of your trust in God?

a) In this regard, what does it look like for you to develop endurance? What are some of the things you can do to ensure you have enough perseverance to bring you to the fulfilment of God's promises?

END NOTE

Chapter 20:

THE UNEXPECTED THINGS ARE NOW EXPECTED

"I have said these things to you,
that in me you may have peace.
In the world you will have tribulation.
But take heart; I have overcome the world!"
(John 16:33 ESV).

The context of this verse is that it takes place during the Lord's farewell speech to His disciples (John 13–16). A rather appropriate backdrop to the end note of this book! But that's not why I chose it. I chose it because it contains a suitable concluding reflection.

Jesus tells His disciples that He's leaving them and is getting them ready for what is about to happen – both to Him and to them as His followers.

With His death on the cross now imminent, Jesus knows that His disciples are about to face many challenges, so He prepares them by giving them parting instructions and reassurances. They'll need to draw on these for the season of persecution they're about to be thrust into when their faith will be severely tested.

Jesus doesn't sugarcoat the challenges that they'll soon be facing. He tells them plainly that because they are His witnesses, they will be hated, beaten, killed and experience great sorrow (John 15:18; 20; 16:1–4; 20).

But He also calms them with many reassurances. He reminds them that He loves them, will always be with them in the person of His Spirit, whom He will send to help and guide them in all things and tells them that they will have great joy (John 14:18; 25; 15:9; 16:20).

The Lord finishes his speech by saying:

> I've told you all this, so that trusting me, you will be unshakable and assured, deeply at peace. In this godless world, you will continue to experience difficulties. But take heart! I've conquered the world (John 16:33 MSG).

Although this verse is spoken by Jesus to His apostles, these words still apply to believers today. For here the Lord gives us timeless biblical truths that place a most appropriate full stop on the message of this book.

The Lord tells His disciples to expect hardships. And He relates these difficulties directly to the condition of this world. We know that the condition of our world is still steeped in godlessness (John 12:31; 2 Cor 4:4; Eph 2:2; 1 John 5:19). The effects of this godlessness are evident. Sin and its consequences abound in our daily lives. We still "continue to experience difficulties" – there is no escaping that until the Lord returns (Rev 21:4).

The unexpected things are now expected. Some of the challenges we will face will certainly be the result of persecution for the sake of the gospel, just like the original disciples Jesus first spoke these words to. At other times, they will be challenges of a different kind, much like those we have discussed in this book. Irrespective of the cause, we will continue to meet with challenges in this life because of the fallen condition of this world.

But notice how the Lord almost skips over this fact by bookending it with both His peace and victory (two more timeless truths). By doing so, He takes our focus off the reality of hardships and places all the emphasis on the greater truth of who He is and what He has done for us. We must not miss this deliberate shift of perspective, for it gives us the key to surviving the unexpected things with unshakable faith.

The Lord invites us to change our perspective about the challenges we will experience in this life. And the lens He gives us is Himself – Jesus Christ, who is both Lord and Messiah (Acts 2:36)! The Lord unveils a profound truth for us when it comes to developing tenacious faith. He shows us that we have no reason to dread the hardships we will meet in this world because He has made full provision for us to overcome them.

The Lord reminds us not to give any power to the unexpected things we will encounter. We must take care that we do not make idols of our hardships and let them become the heroes in our story. An idol is anything we place before God. When we place our attention continually on our difficulties, we end up worshipping them with our time, focus and energy. We unwittingly make them the hero.

The shift in emphasis in John 16:33, while subtle and easily missed at first, is deliberate on the Lord's part. He reminds us to place the unexpected things, the many difficult challenges we will face in this world, in the right place – behind Him. Jesus is the hero. He is the hero of our dot journey and not the unexpected things. When we meet a difficulty, we don't place the emphasis on it. Instead, we place the emphasis on Jesus Christ and on what He has already done and the victory He has secured for us.

This is how we strip the unexpected things of their power to weaken our faith. This is how we keep persevering in faith and enlarging our capacity to endure hardships (2 Pet 1:8). We keep our focus on the truth greater than our hardship – the truth of who Jesus is and what He has done for us.

Our focus should always be on the greater truth of Jesus Christ, not the reality of the troubles themselves. This is what the Lord reminds us of. If we shift our perspective and put the emphasis in the right place, we establish ourselves in a faith that endures – right until the end (Heb 3:14).

The two bookends of His peace and victory are important. They are two tracks for us to travel on during times of difficulty: the track of His peace on the one side and the track of His victory on the other.

The track of His peace allows us to encounter the unexpected things with supernatural peace. It's a peace that transcends our comprehension because it's perfect, just as Jesus is perfect:

> Peace I leave with you; *my peace* I give to you. Not as the world gives do I give to you. Let not your hearts be troubled, neither let them be afraid (John 14:27 ESV).

Jesus gives us *His* peace. It's a peace that isn't born of man, but God:

> ...do not be anxious about anything, but in everything by prayer and supplication with thanksgiving let your requests be made known to God. And *the peace of God*, which surpasses all

> understanding, will guard your hearts and your minds in Christ Jesus (Phil 4:6–7 ESV).

It's a peace we don't have to strive to keep ourselves in. He keeps us in it by His power, as we continually put our faith and trust in Him: "You keep him in perfect peace whose mind is stayed on you, because he trusts in you" (Isa 26:3 ESV).

Praise Jesus for giving us His perfect peace! His peace rips the mask of fear off the face of our trials. He gives us His perfect peace to rest in. No matter how frightening our circumstances might appear, they are no match for the peace of God; He is the Prince of Peace (Isa 9:6). Recall how Jesus slept in the boat that was caught in a raging storm (Matt 8:23–27). What a wonderful support we have in His perfect peace!

The other track, the track of His victory, assures us that beyond the unpleasantness of our situation lies only one conclusion – we overcome. In Christ, we have already overcome this world (Rom 8:17). This means we don't need to work out our own plan to help us through what we're facing. Rather, we remain assured that our enduring partnership with His Spirit is continually moving us toward only one determined end:

> For everyone who has been born of God overcomes the world. And this is the victory that has overcome the world—our faith. Who is it that overcomes the world except the one who believes that Jesus is the Son of God? (1 John 5:4–5 ESV).

We overcome to receive His victory. We do this through faith, the kind of faith that endures until we receive the fulfilment of His promises, the kind that is fully convinced of the certain victory we've obtained through Jesus Christ.

Notice what 1 John 5:4 tells us – we overcome by *our faith*! Can you now see why the devil is out to weaken and destroy our faith through the unexpected things?

God's enemy wants to use hardship to rock our faith and trust in God's goodness. The devil knows that if he can cast doubt on God's goodness, if he can twist God's image, we won't be able to endure in faith to the end. Therefore, we are exhorted to:

> Be prepared. You're up against far more than you can handle on your own. Take all the help you can get, every weapon God has issued, so that when it's all over but the shouting, you'll still be on your feet. Truth, righteousness, peace, faith and salvation are more than words. Learn how to apply them. You'll need them throughout your life. God's Word is an *indispensable* weapon. In the same way, prayer is essential in this ongoing warfare. Pray hard and long. Pray for your brothers and sisters. Keep your eyes open. Keep each other's spirits up so that no one falls behind or drops out (Eph 6:13–18 MSG).

In John 16:33, the Lord takes the emphasis off the many hardships we will face in this world and places it on the greater truth of who He is and what He has done for us. More specifically, he gives us two proven tracks to travel through the unexpected things on: His perfect peace and secured victory.

Who is Jesus Christ and what has He done for you? What does His perfect peace feel like in the midst of the storms of life? What is the victory we have in Him? That is the topic of another book, one that I'm thankful I don't have to write, for it has already been written.

The book is titled the Bible and it is authored by the Holy Spirit. You can read all about who Jesus is and what He's done for you there. If you are new to this book, I encourage you to begin by reading John, but before you do so, I invite you to pray this simple prayer: "Jesus Christ, reveal the truth of who you are and what you have done for me as I read your word. Amen."

Expected, But Not Yet Fully Understood

While the unexpected things can now be expected, they aren't always easily understood from this side of eternity. The chasm between the known and unknown remains. Consequently, the trials we face in our lives for now remain puzzling.

Although they might continue to be confusing, the unexpected things need no longer be the places in which our faith fails and we stop trusting in God. He has already made full provision for us in these times.

We should be safeguarding a faith that is steadfast and immovable, one that will bring us through the confusing fog of the unexpected things with our faith intact.

We began our journey together seeking a way to do just that – preparing our faith for the hard places. I asked you to engage your imagination and do a simple join-the-dots activity that can help us to look at our lives and our difficulties a little differently. I hope that through reading this book and working through the exercises, you've begun to train your faith to view the unexpected things through the eyes of eternity, rather than your own limitations.

I can think of no better way to sum up our journey together than with the lyrics of a song from one of my favourite movies, *The Prince of Egypt*. The song was written by Stephen Schwartz and is titled, *Through Heaven's Eyes*:

A single thread in a tapestry –
Though its colour brightly shines –
Can never see its purpose
In the pattern of the grand design.
And the stone that sits on the very top
Of the mountain's mighty face.
Does it think it's more important
Than the stones that form the base?
So how can you see what your life is worth
Or where your value lies?
You can never see through the eyes of man.
You must look at your life,
Look at your life through heaven's eyes.
Lai-la-lai...
A lake of gold in the desert sand
Is less than a cool fresh spring.
And to one lost sheep, a shepherd boy
Is greater than the richest king.
If a man lose ev'rything he owns,
Has he truly lost his worth?
Or is it the beginning
Of a new and brighter birth?
So how do you measure the worth of a man
In wealth or strength or size?
In how much he gained or how much he gave?
The answer will come,
The answer will come to him who tries
To look at his life through heaven's eyes.
And that's why we share all we have with you,
Though there's little to be found.
When all you've got is nothing,

There's a lot to go around.
No life can escape being blown about
By the winds of change and chance.
And though you never know all the steps,
You must learn to join the dance.
You must learn to join the dance.
Lai-la-lai...
So how do you judge what a man is worth?
By what he builds or buys?
You can never see with your eyes on earth.
Look through heaven's eyes.
Look at your life,
Look at your life,
Look at your life through heaven's eyes!

AND SO, THE END...

Friends, my hope is that you will leave this book with these three big takeaways:

1. Expect the unexpected things. They are as inevitable in this life as death and taxes.

2. Plan for the unplanned. We should prepare our faith to meet with and prevail through the unexpected things. This preparation means we must equip our faith with the tools it needs to develop and increase in endurance.

3. Know that the fog will eventually clear. Determine to press through the unexpected things and make it all the way to your final dot.

The three handles I've given you in this book are by no means exhaustive. How can they be? We've been given far more through Jesus Christ (2 Pet 1:4). The handles of partnership, perspective and perseverance aren't something formulaic and mechanical, but are wholly relational.

These three handles are rooted in our relationship with Jesus Christ. It's only through intimate relationship with Him that we're able to give Him our ongoing cooperation and see the greater purpose beyond our present suffering. Lastly, through our relationship with the Lord, we can persevere through trials, so that we'll still be waiting for Him when He returns. It's all found in intimacy with Jesus.

If you don't yet know the Lord, I invite you to get into relationship with Him by accepting Him as your Lord and

Saviour. The untold joy of His intimacy, grace and love awaits you on the other side of a simple prayer of faith found on the opposite page.

Perhaps you're already a believer, but recognise that the relationship you have with Jesus is not as intimate as it could be. You're not enjoying the spiritual fruit that can only be found in that intimacy. I invite you to pray this short prayer:

Lord, I want to be in intimate relationship with you.
It's the type of relationship you have called me to.
Forgive me for what I've made it.
I choose from this day forward to keep drawing closer to you.
Help me to keep you at the centre of my life in all I do.
In your name, I pray.
Amen.

Lastly, I pray for all of us that our faith will not fail and that we'll all make it to our very last dot, in Jesus' name.

A Closing Appeal

Dear precious and beloved child of God, we must make it to the end with Jesus! We cannot allow our faith to come to a stop anywhere before that point – what a tragedy this would be! We must do everything possible to ensure that our faith in Christ doesn't end up on the shipwrecked shores of abandoned faith. Moreover, we must do everything possible to help those around us escape these shores, too.

I bless you to remain steadfast and immovable in your faith in Jesus Christ until the very end.

Lord Jesus, I acknowledge that I am a sinner.
I ask you to forgive me for my sins.
I believe you are the only Son of God and that you died on the cross for my sins.
Please, come and live in my heart as I surrender my life to you.
I choose from this day forward to live for you and to walk in your ways.
I acknowledge that I need your help daily in this process.
I pray this in your name, Jesus Christ.
Amen.

WORKS CITED

1. Brown, Gregory. 2021. "9. Consequences of Sin." Bible.org, 9 December 2021. https://bible.org/seriespage/9-consequences-sin
2. Boyd, Gregory A. 1998. "After the Order of Melcheizedek, Part 2." Podcast, 28:33. Woodland Hills Church. https://whchurch.org/sermon/after-the-order-of-melchizedek-part-2/
3. Oxford Learner's Dictionaries. 2023. "Cooperation"Oxfordlearnersdictionaries.com, 9 May 2023. https://www.oxfordlearnersdictionaries.com/definition/american_english/cooperation
4. eNCA. 2020. "SA Lockdown: Bridal couple and guests arrested on their wedding day." YouTube, 5 April 2020. https://www.youtube.com/watch?v=60e79d0t8Q0
5. Karrim, Azarrah and Madia, Tshidi. 2020."Ramaphosa summonses Ndabeni-Abrahams to a meeting over lockdown lunch." News24, 7 April 2020. https://www.news24.com/news24/ramaphosa-summonses-ndabeni-abrahams-to-a-meeting-over-lockdown-lunch-20200407
6. Zodhiates, Spiros., Warren Baker, and Eugene Carpenter.2018. "Lord" In Complete Word Study Dictionary: OT and NT for E-Sword. E-Sword X Version 8.0.1. (29).
7. Malick, David. 2004. "An Introduction to the Book of Judges." Bible. Org, 10 June 2004. https://bible.org/article/introduction-book-judges.
8. Heater, Homer Jr. 2021. "2. Judges." Bible.Org, 21 December 2021. https://bible.org/seriespage/2-judges.
9. Vocabulary.Com Dictionary. 2023. "Perspective" Vocabulary.com, 25 April 2023. https://www.vocabulary.com/dictionary/Perspective
10. The Bible Project. "Job". Wisdom Series, 21 April 2023. https://bibleproject.com/explore/video/job/

11. Barry, John D., Douglas Mangum, Derek R. Brown, Michael S. Heiser, Miles Custis, Elliot Ritzema, Matthew M. Whitehead, Michael R. Grigoni, and David Bomar. 2012, 2016. Faithlife Study Bible. Bellingham, WA: Lexham Press.

12. DeSisto, Austin. "NS-16 New Shepard." Everyday Astronaut, 21 July 2021. https://everydayastronaut.com/ns-16-new-shepard-2/

13. Oxford Languages. 2023. "Recovery" Google.com, 9 May 2023.

https://theculturetrip.com/africa/south-africa/articles/18-south-african-slang-words-and-phrases-you-should-know/

https://www.google.com/search?q=def%3A+recovery&oq=def%3A+recovery&aqs=chrome..69i57j69i58.5757j0j7&sourceid=chrome&ie=UTF-8

14. Merriam-Webster Dictionary. 2023. "Purpose" Merriam-Webster.com, 10 May 2023. https://www.merriam-webster.com/dictionary/purpose#:~:text=%3A%20something%20set%20up%20as%20an,purpose

15. Oxford Languages. 2023. "Perseverance." Google.com, 6 June 2023. https://www.google.com/search?q=def%3Aperseverance&oq= def%3Aperseverance&aqs=chrome..69i57j69i58.3005j0j15&sourceid=chrome&ie=UTF-8

16.Van Cleave, Nathaniel M. 1991. "Isaiah". In Spirit Filled Life Bible, NKJV, 999. Thomas Nelson Publishers: Nashville.

17. Brown, Gregory. 2017. "12. Experiencing God's Promises (Genesis 21) | Bible.Org." Bible.Org. July 10, 2017. https://bible.org/seriespage/12-experiencing-god-s-promises-genesis-21.

18. Macpherson, Alex. 2020. "Ostapenko powers to Roland Garros title out of left field in 2017." Wtatennis.com, 30 May 2020.

https://www.wtatennis.com/news/1675152/ostapenko-powers-to-roland-garros-title-out-of-left-field-in-2017

19. Jamieson, Robert, A. R. Fausset, and David Brown. 1997. Commentary Critical and Explanatory on the Whole Bible. Oak Harbour, WA: Logos Research Systems, Inc.